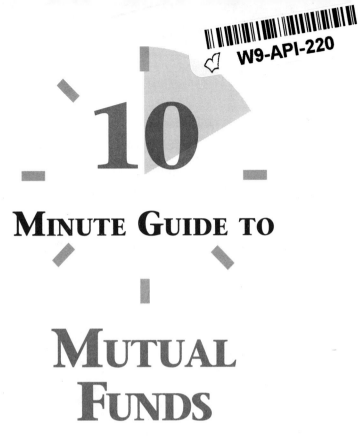

10

MINUTE GUIDE TO

MUTUAL FUNDS

by Werner Renberg

alpha books

Macmillan Spectrum/Alpha Books

A Division of Macmillan General Reference
A Simon & Schuster Macmillan Company
1633 Broadway, New York, NY 10019-6785

To Dan and Roz, Gil, and our first grandchild, Aaron

Copyright©1996 by Werner Renberg

International Standard Book Number: 0-02-861284-1
Library of Congress Catalog Card Number: 96-68540

98 97 96   8 7 6 5 4 3 2 1

Interpretation of the printing code: the rightmost double-digit number is the year of the book's first printing; the rightmost single-digit number is the number of the book's printing. For example, a printing code of 96-1 shows that this copy of the book was printed during the first printing of the book in 1996.

Printed in the United States of America

Publisher: Theresa Murtha
Development Editor: Debra Wishik Englander
Production Editors: Michael Thomas, Whitney Ward
Copy Editor: Geneil Breeze
Cover Designer: Dan Armstrong
Designer: Barbara Kordesh
Production Team: Heather Butler, Angela Calvert, Cindy Fields, Laure Robinson

CONTENTS

INTRODUCTION

If you're like many other people in similar circumstances—similar means, similar needs, similar dreams—you may react in a similar way to the thought of investing in mutual funds:

- You have heard or read that investing in stock, bond, and/or money market funds could help you to earn more income, accumulate a sum of money, or both.

- You have the impression that it would take a lot more money than you have—and more than the minimums that funds require—to buy enough different securities to have an adequately diversified portfolio.

- You are intimidated by the notion of having to choose from the large number of mutual funds in existence, don't know where to begin to find funds that could be right for you, and may be reluctant to hire somebody to advise you because you don't know whom to trust or cannot afford the fee that an adviser might charge.

This book is for you.

In 20 lessons, each of which should take you about 10 minutes to digest, you can learn enough to start acting as your own money manager.

You may still prefer to turn to a broker or other salesperson, for one reason or another, and pay the necessary commissions or fees, but you owe it to yourself to understand enough about the subject so that you will have no doubts about what is recommended to you—or that, if you do have doubts, you can question the recommendations with confidence.

How This Book Is Organized

The first three lessons cover the broad subject of mutual funds—from the definition through their potential long-term rewards and short-term risks.

The next four deal with the steps you need to take to decide which types of funds would be appropriate for you: determining your investment objectives and tolerance for short-term volatility, appropriate allocation of your financial assets, and formulation of your investment strategy.

Lessons 8 through 15 deal with the various broad groups of mutual fund categories: money market funds, taxable and tax-exempt bond funds, equity funds, and mixed assets funds.

Whichever category or categories of funds you decide to invest in, you need to know certain things that apply to all. These are addressed in the final five lessons. They include pointers about getting and studying the information from fund companies to aid you in making your selections, deciding whether to pay sales loads (or charges) or go for no-load funds, determining the levels of annual expenses that funds may absorb, monitoring your fund investments during the years that you own them, and switching among funds as it becomes necessary or desirable.

As you master these facets of mutual fund investing, you will soon see that the subject need not be intimidating at all—that you can develop the self-confidence needed to use funds to achieve your investment goals without exposing yourself to any more risk than you are able or willing to accept.

Conventions Used in This Book

The following icons will help you find your way around the *10 Minute Guide to Mutual Funds:*

Tip   Tip icons signify useful ideas to help save time and/or avoid confusion.

Plain English   Plain English sidebars define new or unfamiliar terms in (you got it) "plain English."

Panic Button   Panic Button icons identify potential trouble areas.

ACKNOWLEDGMENTS

I wish to acknowledge the guidance of my editor, Debby Englander, who inspired me to present the material in a novel way to accommodate the many who prefer to assimilate information pertaining to a possibly intimidating subject in easily digestible bites, and the support of my wife, Dalia, who accepted greater demands on her time to ensure the smooth functioning of our household during the months that this book demanded so much of mine.

In dedicating this book to our sons, daughter-in-law, and first grandchild, I do so in the hope that the economy inherited by their generations will flourish sufficiently to enable all to share in its bounty—and that policy makers in government, business, and labor will do all in their power to prevent the revival of serious inflation that could severely impact the living standard enjoyed by all of us.

DEFINING MUTUAL FUNDS

In this lesson, you learn what mutual funds are and how you can benefit by investing in them.

WHAT IS A MUTUAL FUND?

A mutual fund is a type of investment company that you can choose to earn additional income, to accumulate a nest egg for your retirement or other long-term goals, or both. Unlike investing directly in individual stocks and bonds, when you invest in a mutual fund, you are investing in a variety of stocks, bonds, and/or money market securities.

 Mutual Fund An investment company that enables you to pool your money with that of other people for investment in a portfolio of stocks, bonds, or other securities, toward a common objective.

Mutual funds have become very popular. About one of every three U.S. households now owns one or more of the 6,000 mutual funds in operation, according to the Investment

Company Institute. A decade ago, one of every five U.S. house-holds owned mutual funds and had fewer than 2,000 funds to choose from.

WHY FUNDS ARE SO POPULAR

There are several reasons for the popularity of mutual funds. The key factors are:

- *Professional management.* Relying on a fund portfolio manager's expertise in knowing which securities to buy or sell makes sense for many investors, particularly if you haven't the time or inclination to research investments.

- *Ease of investing.* You can invest in a mutual fund with a few thousand dollars or less. If you make your own investment decisions and deal directly with a fund company, you don't need to pay anyone a commission.

- *Simplicity of transactions.* You can easily buy or sell your fund shares by mail, telephone, or wire. Also, certain funds allow you to write checks against your fund accounts.

INSTANT DIVERSIFICATION FOR SMALL AMOUNTS

One of the most important features of mutual funds is the legally mandated diversification they provide you to reduce investment risk.

Diversification   Diversification is the practice of owning the securities of different issuers, thereby limiting the share of a fund's assets that any one of them may represent. This makes it less likely that you would suffer a major loss than if you owned only one stock and it lost value.

By investing only a few thousand dollars—less if you sign up for a regular investment plan available through some fund companies—you achieve instant diversification. You would have to invest a lot more money to buy enough different individual stocks, bonds, or money market securities to achieve a satisfactory level of diversification.

WHY THEY ARE CALLED OPEN-END COMPANIES

Mutual funds create and issue new shares when you invest and redeem your shares when you sell, thereby reducing the number of shares that they have outstanding. That's why mutual funds are formally referred to as *open-end investment companies.* They differ from *closed-end funds,* whose shares you buy from, or sell to, other investors through a broker.

Open-End   Funds that are continually issuing new shares and redeeming outstanding shares. Closed-end funds also are invested in portfolios of securities, but they have fixed numbers of shares outstanding that are publicly traded. They are not redeemable.

GETTING YOUR MONEY OUT

Compared to some other investments, you can sell your mutual fund shares easily. Under the Investment Company Act of 1940, which provides for the regulation of funds by the U.S. Securities and Exchange Commission (SEC), you can get your money out of a fund whenever you request a redemption of shares (except in rare circumstances, when the SEC may permit a temporary suspension of your redemption right).

HOW YOU ARE—AND AREN'T—PROTECTED

The SEC, of course, cannot ensure that you will get back as much money as you put in. The 1940 Act was intended to protect you against unscrupulous mutual fund managements, not against a decline in the bond or stock market or against a manager's poor securities selections.

Similarly, the federal law that insures your bank deposits doesn't protect you against losing money because of a market drop or inferior fund management when you buy mutual fund shares from a bank.

DETERMINING THE VALUES OF MUTUAL FUND SHARES

Whether you're buying or redeeming shares in a fund, the price that you pay or receive is based on its *net asset value* (NAV) per share.

Net Asset Value (NAV) The value of one share's interest in a fund's net assets.

A fund's NAV is calculated by adding up its total assets, subtracting its total liabilities, and dividing the resulting net assets by the number of shares outstanding.

This calculation must be performed every day that U.S. securities markets are open. It is done after the markets close, when the day's closing values for a fund's securities can be determined and when the day's purchase and redemption requests from investors have been added up.

What You Pay or Receive for a Share

You can buy or redeem the shares of many funds at their NAVs—that is, without paying a sales charge (or *load*)—by dealing directly with the fund companies that sponsor them. Such funds are known as *no-load funds*.

Load The sales charge that may be added to the NAV when you buy a fund's shares or subtracted from your proceeds when you sell them.

No-Load Fund Almost any fund whose shares you can buy or sell without paying a sales charge.

Other funds, referred to as *load funds*, may impose sales charges of as much as 5% or more of the offering prices at which shares may be purchased. Loads may be added to NAVs when you buy from a broker, banker, financial planner, or other salesperson, or they may be deferred until you sell, when they're subtracted from your proceeds.

THREE BROAD CLASSES OF FUNDS

Mutual funds are classified according to the types of securities they own, their investment objectives, and the investment policies they follow in trying to realize them.

Funds are first divided into three broad classes based on the types of financial assets that they primarily hold:

- *Money market funds* own U.S. Treasury bills and/or other high-quality government or corporate securities that mature in a few months.

- *Bond funds* may primarily own bonds and other debt securities, maturing in 1 to 30 years, issued by federal, state, local, or foreign governments, by U.S. or foreign corporations.

- *Equity funds* are principally invested in common stocks of U.S. and foreign corporations.

DIVIDING FUNDS ACCORDING TO TAXABILITY

Money market and bond funds are also divided into taxable and tax-exempt funds. Taxable funds distribute income dividends that are taxable by federal and state governments, whereas tax-exempt funds pay dividends exempt from federal income tax because the funds are invested in state and local government securities. (However, tax-exempt funds may be subject to state tax.)

Dividing Funds According to Investment Objectives

Bond funds and equity funds are classified into a number of categories according to their investment objectives and policies, and, thus, according to degrees and types of investment risk. By understanding how funds are classified and limiting your search to those in groups suitable for you, you should be able to avoid funds that are too risky. If you're willing to take on higher risk funds in the hope of higher returns, you can find those funds as well.

In this lesson, you learned what mutual funds are and how you can benefit by investing in them. In the next lesson, you learn the potential long-term rewards of investing in mutual funds.

THE LONG-TERM REWARDS OF MUTUAL FUNDS

In this lesson, you learn about the potential rewards that you may earn by keeping your investments in mutual funds for many years.

THERE ARE NO GUARANTEES

Nobody can guarantee that your mutual fund investment will grow by a certain amount over a given time period. This is because the performance of the funds depends largely on the rise and fall of the prices of the money market issues, bonds, and stocks that they own. And nobody can predict where prices of any of these securities will be at any point in time, except for money market issues and bonds whose prices will equal their face values when they mature.

Fund performance also depends—to a lesser but still important degree—on the costs they incur.

IT'S NOT LIKE PUTTING MONEY IN A BANK

Investing in funds with fluctuating prices and varying rates of return is not like putting money into a bank's savings account or certificate of deposit (CD). The principal values of a savings account or a CD don't go down, and the yield is usually fixed. You know how much compounded interest you'll earn, and you also know the possible penalty for early withdrawal.

Nevertheless, investing in one or more well-managed, suitable mutual funds is often a sound financial strategy, enabling you over time to earn more than you could earn on money in the bank.

ARE MUTUAL FUNDS AS SAFE AS MONEY IN A BANK?

Although the shares of mutual funds are not federally insured, their safety record, which depends on sound portfolio management and compliance with federal law and regulations, has generally been impressive. Cases of funds which are so poorly managed that investors suffered major losses have been rare in modern times.

USING HISTORIC DATA TO PROJECT POTENTIAL PERFORMANCE

To get a sense of how much your money could grow when you invest in a mutual fund, you need to look first at historic performance for the classes of securities that the fund owns. You will find the data, such as those of Standard & Poor's or Frank Russell Company for stocks and Lehman Brothers or Salomon Brothers for bonds, in reference works at a nearby library.

Past performance does not guarantee an absolute level of future performance, but the data do give you a sense of relative performance. They tell you which types of securities have rewarded investors more than others over time.

For example, the least risky securities—money market instruments—have provided the lowest rates of return. Nevertheless, they have kept investors whole against inflation since the early 1980s, slightly exceeding the consumer price index (CPI) most of the time.

More risky securities—bonds and stocks—have provided returns that were a little (bonds) or a lot (stocks) higher.

MEASURING INVESTMENT PERFORMANCE

Before sizing up the performance of various investments—whether individual securities or shares of mutual funds—you have to become familiar with the most common yardstick used to measure it. This is known as *total return*.

> **Total Return**   The rate of growth (or decline) in the value of an investment. Whether the percentage is calculated for individual securities or mutual funds, reinvestment of income (in additional securities or fund shares) is assumed. When total return is calculated for mutual funds, reinvestment of capital gains distributions is also assumed.

You'll be using total return data often, when you're considering which funds to invest in and when you're evaluating the performance of the funds that you own. You'll find them not only in mutual fund reports to shareholders but also in newspapers' fund tables and other media.

When you see total return data, be sure you understand the period for which they reflect performance. When you compare funds' returns with one another or with those of other invest-ment vehicles, you want total returns expressed as annual rates, not in cumulative terms. A 100% total return over five years—doubling investors' money—translates into a 14.9% annual rate. Not bad, but not as impressive as a 100% cumula-tive return.

Total return reflects the sum of two types of data:

- The rise or fall in the price of a stock, bond, or mu-tual fund share.

- Income from dividends or interest, as reinvested in additional stocks, bonds, or fund shares.

As you can see, total return is more meaningful than just price change alone. By taking income into consideration, total re-turn includes what often is a significant contributor to what you can earn.

Moreover, it puts various types of funds—those whose returns come primarily from appreciation and those whose returns come primarily from income—on a comparable basis.

USING TOTAL RETURN DATA

Because the performance of any type of mutual fund for a pe-riod as short as a year is not very meaningful, it is important to look at total returns for longer periods.

The SEC requires a fund's management, when advertising per-formance, to provide the fund's annual rates of total return for five and ten years (or for the lifetime of the fund, if it's new) as well as for one year.

By comparing rates for one, five, and ten years, you can quickly get an idea of whether a fund's returns have been vola-tile or consistently good (or poor).

HISTORIC RETURNS FOR MAJOR CLASSES OF SECURITIES

Looking at historic returns for the major classes of securities, you find:

- Stocks, the most risky securities, have done the best on the average. In the five and ten years ending with 1995, the U.S. stock market had average annual total returns of 16.6% and 14.9%, respectively, as measured by the Standard & Poor's 500 Composite Stock Price Index.

- Bonds followed, with the total U.S. taxable investment grade bond market, as measured by the Salomon Brothers Broad Investment Grade Bond Index, recording average annual returns of 9.6% and 9.7%, respectively for the two periods.

Investment Grade Bond   A bond judged by a rating agency, such as Moody's Investors Service or Standard & Poor's, to have high or good credit quality.

- Money market instruments lagged. The safest of all, U.S. Treasury bills, had average annual returns of 3.9% and 5.2%, respectively, over the five and ten years, according to CDA/Wiesenberger.

All classes of securities, on the average, beat inflation, which averaged 2.8% for the five-year period and 3.5% for the ten-year period.

Whatever the future may bring in levels of returns, those relationships are not likely to change.

MUTUAL FUNDS' SHORT-TERM RISK

In this lesson, you learn about the short-term risk of investing in bond and equity funds.

WHAT IS SHORT-TERM RISK?

When you wonder about the risk of investing in mutual funds, you are probably thinking about the short-term risk of losing money. With rare exceptions, funds have tended to have positive long-term total returns.

> **Short-Term** Depending on the use, it may refer to periods of from a year or less to three (or even five) years.

What then is the short-term risk of investing in a fund? Is it that you could quickly lose all your money, as if you were betting on a horse? No, not at all. It's that you could lose some of your money, if you sold a fund's shares a short time after you bought them and their price had fallen to less than you paid.

This is unlikely to happen (but not impossible) with money market funds, which are managed to maintain stable NAVs of $1 a share, but not at all unlikely with equity and bond funds.

HOW FUNDS HAVE PERFORMED

On the average, the broad classes of mutual funds sometimes exceeded and sometimes lagged the average performance of the broad classes of securities in the periods ending with 1995, but their returns also consistently beat inflation, as table 2.1 shows.

TABLE 2.1 HOW BROAD CLASSES OF SECURITIES AND MUTUAL FUNDS PERFORMED AND COMPARED WITH INFLATION IN 1, 5, AND 10 YEARS ENDING IN 1995

SECURITIES/FUND CATEGORY	ANNUAL RATES OF TOTAL RETURN		
	1995	1991-95	1986-95
Common stocks	37.6%	16.6%	14.9%
General equity funds	31.1	17.0	13.2
Taxable investment grade bonds	18.5	9.6	9.7
Taxable bond funds	15.2	9.9	8.9
U.S. Treasury bills	4.9	3.9	5.2
Taxable money market funds	5.4	4.1	5.7
Inflation	2.5	2.8	3.5

Sources: CDA/Wiesenberger, Lipper Analytical Services, Salomon Brothers, Standard & Poor's, U.S. Bureau of Labor Statistics.

Leading funds in each general equity fund category achieved five- and ten-year returns substantially higher than the averages of 17.0% and 13.2%, respectively, for all general equity funds, as calculated by Lipper Analytical Services.

In this lesson, you learned about the potential rewards that you may earn by investing in mutual funds for longer periods of time. In the next lesson, you learn about potential short-term risks of mutual funds.

That's why you should consider equity and bond funds as investments for at least five years—probably long enough to include a recovery as well as a down market, in case a down market does occur.

TAKING SHORT-TERM DROPS IN STRIDE

When you invest in well-managed equity or bond funds for the long run, you should be able to take short-term drops in stride and not lose sleep over them.

This is particularly true of equity funds, which can experience a short-term plunge but bounce back and appreciate considerably over time as stock prices rise to reflect the growth of corporate profits in a growing U.S. economy.

To cite an extreme case, some people may have thought that the world had come to an end when the stock market had a record fall of more than 20% in one day: October 19, 1987. Although not completely forgotten, that "crash" receded in memory as the market returned to its previous level in a year and went on to new heights.

Bond funds are a different story. They won't go up very much, unless interest rates are in a downward trend. On the other hand, they probably won't go down much either, unless inflation becomes severe and interest rates take off again.

tip   **Be Patient**   To reduce the risk of losing money on a fund investment, be patient and hold on to your shares through market ups and downs—provided that you're convinced you've chosen a good fund.

To put it simply, you can draw two conclusions:

- You can't be sure that the NAV of either an equity or a bond fund will match or exceed your cost if you hold its shares for a long time.

- The odds that it will do so are greater than if you hold them only a year or two.

USING TOTAL RETURN TO MEASURE SHORT-TERM RISK

The level of short-term risk that an investment in an equity or bond fund involves is often described in terms of how much or how little the fund's total returns fluctuate.

Risk   A complex term that refers to the likelihood that you can lose money when one or more factors cause an investment's value to decline.

One way financial analysts commonly define a fund's risk level is in terms of the volatility of its monthly total returns over the most recent 36 months—that is, how much the returns rise above and fall below the average for the period.

FLUCTUATION IN NAV VERSUS TOTAL RETURN

Measures of volatility (or risk) focus on the fluctuation of total returns—not NAVs. Changes in NAVs can overstate a fund's volatility.

You'll recall from Lesson 2 that the total return of a mutual fund is defined as the percentage of the rise or fall in the value

of an investment in a fund, calculated with the assumption that all income and capital gains distributions are reinvested in additional shares.

Distribution   Funds must pay shareholders each year what they have left after expenses from the income they earn on their investments and the net capital gains they realize from the sales of securities. These payments are called distributions.

False Alarm   Don't be alarmed if a fund's NAV went down a lot one day even though the market was calm or up. The NAV could have been reduced to reflect a distribution.

Although both a fund's NAV and its total return change almost every day, in line with the prices of the stocks and/or bonds in its portfolio, the NAV is also marked down to reflect the distributions of dividends and/or capital gains on days when they are credited to shareholders' accounts.

How Much Stocks and Bonds Can Fluctuate in a Month

Most of the time, the month-to-month changes in total returns earned on stocks and bonds are positive. Some of the time, they are large.

Of the 120 months that made up the ten years ending in 1995, stocks had positive returns in 80 months, according to the Standard & Poor's 500 Index; bonds had positive returns in 88 months, according to the Lehman Brothers Aggregate Index.

Tables 3.1 and 3.2 show how much the total returns of stocks and bonds can go up and down in a month.

TABLE 3.1   THE BEST AND WORST MONTHS FOR THE STOCK MARKET 1986–1995

YEAR	TOTAL RETURNS			
	BEST MONTHS		WORST MONTHS	
1986	February	7.5%	September	–8.3%
1987	January	13.5	October	–21.5
1988	February	4.7	August	–3.4
1989	July	9.0	February	–2.5
1990	May	9.8	August	–9.0
1991	December	11.4	June	–4.6
1992	July	4.1	August	–2.1
1993	August	3.8	April	–2.4
1994	August	4.1	March	–4.4
1995	November	4.4	October	–0.4

Source: Standard & Poor's 500 Composite Stock Price Index.

TABLE 3.2   THE BEST AND WORST MONTHS FOR THE BOND MARKET 1986–1995

YEAR	TOTAL RETURNS			
	BEST MONTHS		WORST MONTHS	
1986	February	3.9%	May	–1.9%
1987	October	3.6	April	–2.7
1988	January	3.5	November	–1.2

| | TOTAL RETURNS | | | |
YEAR	BEST MONTHS		WORST MONTHS	
1989	June	3.0	August	–1.5
1990	May	3.0	August	–1.3
1991	December	3.0	June	–0.1
1992	July	2.0	January	–1.4
1993	January	1.9	November	–0.9
1994	July	2.0	March	–2.5
1995	May	3.9	July	–0.2

Source: Lehman Brothers Aggregate Index.

The monthly fluctuations in stocks' total returns usually have been greater than those of bonds. In the ten years, stocks had positive total returns of as much as 13.5% in January 1987 while falling as much as 21.5% in October 1987 (coincidentally, about the same as the drop on that one day, Black Monday).

In their best months of the decade, February 1986 and May 1995, the total returns for bonds didn't get higher than 3.9%. On the other hand, their worst monthly results were no worse than a negative 2.7% in April 1987.

HOW WIDELY SECURITIES AND FUNDS CAN FLUCTUATE IN A YEAR

Tables 3.3 and 3.4 show how much the average total returns of common stocks and bonds—and the funds that own them—have fluctuated on a calendar year basis during the ten years.

Both stock and bond indexes had only one negative year each—stocks being down 3.1% in 1990 and bonds being down 2.9% in 1994—whereas both had a few very good years with stock and bond returns rising as high as 37.6% and 18.5%, respectively, in 1995.

TABLE 3.3   HOW AVERAGE ANNUAL TOTAL RETURNS OF STOCKS AND EQUITY FUNDS HAVE FLUCTUATED 1986–1995

| | **TOTAL RETURNS** | |
YEAR	**COMMON STOCKS**	**EQUITY FUNDS**
1986	18.6%	14.7%
1987	5.1	1.2
1988	16.6	15.8
1989	31.7	24.0
1990	–3.1	–6.3
1991	30.5	35.6
1992	7.6	8.9
1993	10.1	12.5
1994	1.3	–1.7
1995	37.6	31.1

Sources: Common stocks, Standard & Poor's 500 Composite Stock Price Index; general equity funds, Lipper Analytical Services.

The Difference in Years   When studying funds' yearly returns, check whether they refer to calendar years or funds' fiscal years ending in months from January through November. This may help you to make more meaningful comparisons among funds.

Table 3.4 How Average Annual Total Returns of Taxable Bonds and Bond Funds Have Fluctuated 1986–1995

Year	Total Returns	
	Bonds	Bond Funds
1986	15.4%	13.4%
1987	2.6	1.6
1988	8.0	8.5
1989	14.4	10.1
1990	9.1	4.9
1991	16.0	18.1
1992	7.6	7.8
1993	9.9	9.8
1994	–2.9	–3.3
1995	18.5	15.2

Sources: Bonds, Salomon Brothers Broad Investment-Grade Bond Index; taxable fixed income funds, Lipper Analytical Services.

Performance over other 12-month periods ranged even more widely.

Riding Out the Swings Over the Longer Term

By buying average-performing stocks or bonds at the beginning of the decade and holding on throughout the periods of extreme up and down swings, you would have enjoyed annual average total returns, before income taxes and any sales commissions, of 14.9% and 9.7%, respectively.

All stocks and bonds, of course, didn't perform in line with the indexes, and, as Tables 3.3 and 3.4 illustrate, the average equity and bond funds didn't either.

Some funds outperform the indexes, whereas others under-perform them. The difference often lies in the degree of risk to which the funds' investment policies and practices would subject you.

In this lesson, you learned how much short-term risk you could incur by investing in equity or bond funds. In the next lesson, you learn how to formulate your investment objective so that you can pick the right funds.

DETERMINING INVESTMENT OBJECTIVES

In this lesson, you learn how to formulate your investment objective so that you can select mutual funds that meet your needs.

FIGURE OUT WHY YOU'RE INVESTING

You may tell yourself that your priority is "to make money." However, this is too vague as a goal. You need to think about how you want to make money from mutual fund investments. That means thinking through what your goal really is.

In the broadest sense, there are essentially three investment objectives: income; growth (or capital appreciation); and total return—that is, a combination of the two.

SOME QUESTIONS TO ASK YOURSELF

These three are a bit too broad, though. To start the fund selection process, you need to formulate a more specific objective that reflects the rate of return and yield (if any) that you expect as well as the level of risk that you can accept. Fine-tune your objective by asking yourself a few questions, such as:

- Are you only comfortable with lower-risk, lower-return funds in seeking income or growth, even if you are planning to be invested for a good number of years?

- Are you willing and able to take a lot of risk in the hope of earning higher returns that should be—but aren't always—your reward?

Tax-Exempt Income   The income distributions made by a money market or bond fund that invests in state and local government securities whose interest payments are exempt from federal income tax.

- Are you in a high enough federal income tax bracket that you have to think about whether you should be investing to earn federally tax-exempt income?

- Do you have enough income and, therefore, only care about investing to make your money grow to some large amount?

Tax-Deferred Account   An individual retirement account (IRA) or an account in an employer's 401(k) or similar plan that can grow untaxed but from which withdrawals will be taxed.

- Are you planning to invest in a tax-deferred retirement account and, therefore, would consider funds that make large taxable distributions?

- Alternatively, are you planning to invest in a taxable account and, therefore, prefer funds whose distributions are likely to be relatively low?

Formulating Your Investment Objective

As you consider your answers to such questions, your thinking will become more focused, thereby preparing you to identify funds whose investment objectives and policies could make them appropriate for you.

Instead of merely "income," your objective may be maximum income consistent with low, moderate, or high principal risk. Instead of "growth," it may be maximum growth with high risk or moderate growth with lower risk.

Finding Funds Whose Investment Objectives Match Yours

To find funds that feature investment objectives that match yours, you should:

- Determine the investment objective categories in which they are likely to be.

- Screen the funds in these categories to cull out for study those whose investment objectives and policies appear to square with yours.

Although there are around 6,000 money market, bond, and equity funds in operation, it is thus possible—without too much effort—to reduce the number that you should consider to a much smaller, manageable handful in the category or categories of interest to you.

Using the pointers contained in this book, you only really take time to look at funds that seem to be the most suitable.

CLASSIFYING FUNDS ACCORDING TO THEIR OBJECTIVES AND POLICIES

How do you know which fund investment objective categories to research? The SEC requires all registered mutual funds to describe their investment objectives and policies "clearly and concisely" so that investors such as you can easily understand them.

Investment Objective   The goal toward which a mutual fund is managed, such as maximum or moderate (taxable or tax-exempt) income, maximum or moderate growth, and total return.

Investment Policy   The policy followed by a fund to achieve its objective, including the types of securities it may buy and the types and degrees of investment risk it may incur.

On the basis of these descriptions, as well as fund financial statements, funds are classified by firms providing fund performance data, thereby making it easier for you to focus on the fund categories that you've targeted.

HOW MANY INVESTMENT OBJECTIVE CATEGORIES ARE THERE?

How many categories there are depends on who's doing the classifying.

Lipper Analytical Services, a fund performance data firm with the most comprehensive coverage, classifies equity, bond, and mixed assets funds into more than 60 categories, excluding tax-exempt funds limited to investments in single states. (It also created eight categories for money market funds.)

Morningstar Mutual Funds and *The Value Line Mutual Fund Survey,* two biweekly publications, use between 25 and 30 categories for equity, bond, and mixed assets funds. The Investment Company Institute, the industry's principal trade association, classifies such funds into 17 (all excluding money market and single-state tax-exempt funds). Others use still different classification systems.

The Lipper categories (which are used in this book) may be the best known to you because you've probably seen references to them in fund literature and advertisements, in which managements compare their funds' performance with the averages of their peers, and in your daily newspaper, magazines, and other periodicals.

USING THE INVESTMENT OBJECTIVE CATEGORIES

Whichever classification system you find most accessible, direct your attention to the category or categories in which you can expect to find the fund or funds that should meet your needs. If you want taxable income, for example, consider categories of money market and/or bond funds. If you want tax-exempt income, look at tax-exempt money market or bond funds. If you want appreciation, look at one or more categories of equity funds—more aggressive or less aggressive, depending on which you favor. And so on.

In this lesson, you learned how to formulate your own investment objective so that you can select mutual funds that match your needs. In the next lesson, you learn how to think about how much short-term volatility you are able and willing to accept.

How Much Short-Term Volatility Is Acceptable to You?

In this lesson, you learn how to think about how much short-term volatility you are able and willing to accept in trying to achieve your investment objective.

Able, Willing, or Both?

There's a difference between being able to accept short-term volatility and being willing to do so.

If you are investing only for a few years, you may not be able to accept much volatility even though you may be willing to take chances. The bond and/or stock markets—and your funds—could be down just when you want to sell your shares.

If you are investing for a longer period, you may be able to take short-term volatility in stride, but you may not be willing to do it. Whenever you see the stock or bond market drop, you may worry that you're losing money, even if you're invested in good funds that are likely to serve you well over time.

Your Age May Not Be the Most Important Factor

Your age may be an important factor in determining how much short-term risk you should be able and willing to accept, but it isn't the only one. It may not even be the most important one.

To be sure, if you're in your 60s or older, your age would matter because, most likely, you are in, or close to, retirement and less able to recover from a serious loss of principal.

But just because you're in your 60s or older doesn't mean that you have to invest all of your money in bond and money market funds. You may expect to live a good number of years during which inflation will erode the purchasing power of your assets.

-tip- **Remember Inflation** Because you probably will live for many years after you retire, you've got to be aware that even a low rate of inflation will eat into the purchasing power of your money market and bond fund investments.

If you're years away from retirement, you may not want to put all of your money in equity funds, especially if you're planning to sell your shares in a few years, perhaps to buy a house or pay for your children's education.

The Importance of Your Investment Horizon

Clearly, your risk tolerance depends to a high degree on your *investment horizon*—in other words, on how long you plan or expect to be invested to achieve your investment objective.

It's important, therefore, for you to do some planning, taking into consideration a number of factors—including your age, of course—that will help you to conclude how much short-term volatility you can accept.

ONE FUND OR MORE?

When planning your investment strategy in terms of the level of risk that you can tolerate, be aware that you have a greater opportunity to control and adjust your risk exposure when you invest in two or more funds than when you only buy one.

If you want, or can afford, to invest in only one fund, you obviously have to limit yourself to a fund whose expected volatility—whether high or low—is consistent with your investment objective and investment horizon.

If you plan to invest in two or more funds from different investment objective categories, plan in terms of your portfolio's average volatility.

In the simple case of a two-fund portfolio in which each fund accounts for one half, the combination of an above-average-risk fund and a low-risk fund could produce a portfolio blend of average risk.

Average Risk Describes the riskiness of a fund whose level of volatility is about equal to that of a price index for the type of securities that it owns. For domestic equity funds, for example, that's usually the Standard & Poor's 500 Index.

Investing for Income

When investing for income, you may want your fund or funds to have relatively low volatility. This makes sense especially if you need all the money that you get in income distributions and can't afford to reinvest anything.

If you are investing for a longer period and are willing to accept higher risk in the hope of earning higher income, make sure to switch to lower-risk funds as you approach your goal.

The Long and Short of Investing for Total Return or Growth

If your investment objective is total return or growth and you plan to reinvest income and capital gains distributions, your risk tolerance may be higher or lower. It also depends on your investment horizon.

Investing for a Longer Period

You may accept higher volatility in the hope of earning a higher return if you plan to be invested for a longer period.

Of course, if you have limited means and really can't afford to lose money but want to build up a modest sum for retirement or another purpose over a longer period, you should be able to buy low-risk equity funds to meet your needs.

Investing for a Shorter Period

If you are only planning to invest for a short period of time, you should assemble a portfolio of funds with lower volatility—and expect a lower return. This might be a good choice if you:

- Plan to retire in five years or less

- Worry that you may have to take "early" retirement

- Plan to make a major purchase, such as a house or a business, in a few years

- Are saving for college tuition and your child is already in junior or senior high school

In this lesson, you learned how to think about how much short-term volatility you are able and willing to accept. In the next lesson, you learn how to allocate your financial assets among the major asset classes.

ALLOCATING YOUR FINANCIAL ASSETS

In this lesson, you learn how to allocate your total financial assets—that is, your mutual fund holdings and any other investments that you may own—among the major asset classes: stocks, bonds, and cash (or cash equivalents).

Studies have found that investors' decisions as to how much to invest in each class of financial assets play a larger role in determining how well their portfolios of securities perform than choices of specific investments within the asset classes.

Although some analysts may refer to a half dozen or more classes, many usually stick to these three: stocks, bonds, and cash equivalents.

Cash Equivalents Securities regarded as being the equivalents of cash. They may be U.S. Treasury bills or other high-quality money market instruments that usually involve little risk.

TAKING INVENTORY OF YOUR ASSETS

Before considering how your financial assets should be allocated, take inventory of the assets that you own.

If you already own mutual funds, classify money market funds
as cash; classify bond funds and equity funds as bonds and
common stocks, respectively. (The latter funds usually have
some cash, and equity funds also may own some bonds. If the
percentages are small, you may want to ignore them.)

> *tip* **Think of Other Assets**   When thinking of asset
> allocation, don't think only of your present or pro-
> spective mutual funds. If you have other financial
> assets, remember that they, too, can affect your
> financial well-being and should be included in your
> calculations.

In addition to funds, you may have savings accounts (treated
as cash), shares of stock in the company you work for, other
individual common stocks, or bonds, and CDs (which you can
divide according to their maturities, classifying as cash those
maturing in one year or less).

WHY ASSET ALLOCATION MATTERS SO MUCH

What makes asset allocation so important?

When planning to achieve your investment objective in a way
consistent with your risk tolerance, asset allocation is the principal tool for influencing your portfolio's probable long-run
return and short-run volatility.

Stocks have the highest average total returns over the long run, but they also are the most volatile in the short run. Money market instruments have the lowest average returns but are the least volatile. Bonds are in-between.

Thus, a portfolio invested in all three is likely to be less volatile than one invested in stocks alone.

No Asset Class Is the Leader All the Time

Even if common stocks outperform the other asset classes over a period of years, they do not outperform the other two every year. In some years, cash or bonds excel.

To illustrate, common stocks significantly outperformed the other two classes in five of the ten years from 1986 through 1995, as you see in Table 6.1. They were essentially matched by Treasury bills in 1987 and by bonds in 1992 and 1993.

TABLE 6.1   ANNUAL TOTAL RETURNS BY ASSET CLASSES 1986–1995

YEAR	TREASURY BILLS	TAXABLE BONDS	COMMON STOCKS	INFLATION
1986	5.8%	15.4%	18.6%	1.1%
1987	5.2	2.6	5.1	4.4
1988	6.1	8.0	16.6	4.4
1989	7.8	14.4	31.7	4.6
1990	7.3	9.1	–3.1	6.1
1991	5.2	16.0	31.7	3.1

YEAR	TREASURY BILLS	TAXABLE BONDS	COMMON STOCKS	INFLATION
1992	3.2	7.6	7.6	2.9
1993	2.7	9.9	10.1	2.8
1994	3.6	–2.9	1.3	2.7
1995	4.9	18.5	37.5	2.5
1986–1995 Avg.	5.2	9.7	14.9	3.5

Sources: U.S. Treasury bills, CDA/Wiesenberger; Taxable investment grade bonds, Salomon Brothers; Common stocks, Standard & Poor's; Inflation, U.S. Bureau of Labor Statistics.

A portfolio diversified among the three classes—to provide a good return without excessive volatility—makes the most sense for many people—and probably for you too.

COMING UP WITH YOUR TARGETED ASSET MIX

Given the importance of asset allocation, consider what percentages of cash, bonds, and stocks may be right for you and how your (additional) investment in one or more mutual funds would produce the asset mix you're aiming for.

Because it's usually easy to switch among mutual funds, you can simply start with an allocation that seems appropriate for someone in your situation and watch your funds' performance to see if any changes in your allocation are called for. If you are invested in taxable or tax-exempt accounts, however, remember the possible tax consequences of switching out of equity or bond funds: you may realize taxable capital gains when you sell.

SUGGESTED ASSET ALLOCATIONS

To get you started, here are some suggested asset allocations for people in a variety of circumstances:

- If you have a long investment horizon, an allocation of 65%–75% or so to equities and the balance to bond and/or money market funds might be appropriate.

- If you have a short investment horizon, you might hold the equity portion to 25%–35% and put the rest in bond and money market funds.

- If you regard your investment horizon as somewhere in-between, a 50–50 split between equity and non-equity funds might work out well for you.

How you divide the non-equity fund portion between bond and money market funds depends largely on your possible need to take money out without worrying about whether you might be selling shares when they are down and on your need for income.

In this lesson, you learned how to allocate your mutual fund holdings and other financial assets among the major asset classes. In the next lesson, you learn how to plan your total strategy for investing in different types of accounts.

7

PLANNING YOUR TOTAL STRATEGY

In this lesson, you learn how to plan your total investment strategy in the various types of mutual funds that you currently have or are thinking of investing in.

WHAT TYPE OF ACCOUNT?

Whether you're thinking of money market, bond, or equity mutual funds, you also have to think of the types of accounts in which you want to own them. There are essentially three types: taxable, tax-exempt, and tax-deferred.

It's important that you understand the differences, because your total return sooner or later depends on what you have left after paying federal (as well as state and perhaps local) income taxes.

TAXABLE ACCOUNTS

You can be subject to income taxes in any or all of three ways:

- Income distributions by taxable money market, bond, and equity funds are subjected to federal income tax.

- Capital gains distributions from bond and equity funds are taxable at the same rate as income if they are based on short-term gains, but they may be taxed at a lower rate if they are based on long-term gains.

- You must pay taxes on short-term and/or long-term capital gains that you realize when selling shares of bond or equity funds for more than they cost you.

TAX-EXEMPT ACCOUNTS

These are the accounts in which you own shares of federally tax-exempt money market and/or bond funds. In these accounts, you are usually not subject to federal income tax on income distributions, but you may be subject to state income tax unless a fund invests only in securities issued by your state or by your state's local governments. (Federal income tax may be due on tax-exempt interest attributable to what are called *private activity bonds*.)

! **Tax On a Tax-Exempt Fund?**   Income distributed by a tax-exempt bond fund is exempt from federal income tax, but you are subject to federal and state income taxes on the capital gains distributions that you receive from it and/or on the capital gains that you may realize when selling such a fund's shares.

TAX-DEFERRED ACCOUNTS

Tax-deferred accounts include individual retirement accounts (IRAs), which you open on your own; accounts in retirement plans made available to you by your employer, such as Section

401(k) and 403(b) plans, which are named for sections of the Internal Revenue Code; and retirement plans for the self-employed.

You can invest in money market, bond, and/or equity funds in such accounts without having to pay current income tax on income and capital gains distributions that are credited to you.

What's more, you can sell shares of funds held in such accounts without having to worry about paying tax on your capital gains. Unfortunately, if you sell shares at a loss, you cannot ease the pain by applying your realized loss to your ordinary income and reducing your tax bill, as you could in a taxable account.

Whatever their differences, tax-deferred accounts have one thing in common: Your money can grow untaxed until you begin withdrawing it.

YOUR STRATEGY TO MAXIMIZE YOUR RETURNS

Ideally, you want to plan your investment strategy to maximize your return by minimizing your income taxes. When you invest in a money market or bond fund to earn current income or to diversify a growth-oriented portfolio outside a tax-deferred account, you'll have to do some calculations. You have to determine whether you would earn more in a tax-exempt fund than you would have left after paying income tax on income from a taxable fund with similar characteristics.

Of course, if you're investing in a money market or bond fund to diversify a growth-oriented portfolio in a tax-deferred account, you'll only want to buy taxable funds. Tax-exempt fund yields are lower and you'd have to pay taxes on your investments when you withdraw.

If you're investing in equity or mixed assets funds for appreciation or total return and if you have both tax-deferred and taxable accounts, choose the funds with higher yields and rates of capital gains distributions for your tax-deferred accounts and those with lower yields and rates of capital gains distributions in taxable accounts.

In this lesson, you learned how to plan your total investment strategy for the various types of mutual funds. In the next lesson, you learn how to select a money market fund.

HOW TO SELECT A MONEY MARKET FUND

In this lesson, you learn how to select a money market mutual fund that's right for you.

You invest in a money market fund for modest income, safety of principal, and easy access to your money. Income dividends, based on what a fund earns from its investment in government and/or corporate securities, are credited to your account daily and may be paid monthly. You can take them in cash or reinvest them.

THE SAFEST MUTUAL FUNDS—BUT NOT GUARANTEED

Money market funds are the safest form of mutual funds, but they are not 100% safe—even when they are fully invested in U.S. Treasury securities or when they are bought from a bank whose deposit accounts are insured by the government.

The safety of money market funds' principal rests on their investment advisers' ability to manage their portfolios to maintain the funds' NAVs at $1 a share.

The advisers do so primarily in two ways:

- By holding down interest rate risk—and thus volatility. SEC rules require them to limit the weighted average maturities of their portfolios to 90 days.

- By limiting investments to high-quality securities.

STABLE PRINCIPAL BUT FLUCTUATING YIELDS

Although you should be able to rely on sound management to maintain a stable NAV at $1, you cannot rely on a money market fund to have a stable interest rate, as bank passbook savings accounts and CDs do.

A money market fund's yield fluctuates. It can change from one day to the next, depending primarily on changes in the yields of the money market securities that the fund owns.

TWO BROAD CATEGORIES OF MONEY MARKET FUNDS

Money market funds that you can invest in are divided into two broad categories: taxable and tax-exempt.

THREE TYPES OF TAXABLE MONEY MARKET FUNDS

The taxable money market funds are further classified into three groups: those that own only U.S. Treasury securities, which are backed by the full faith and credit of the U.S.; those that may own securities of the Treasury or of federal agencies, some of which may not be similarly backed; and those that may own the securities of corporations, the Treasury, and federal agencies.

Because yields are normally lowest for securities with the highest credit quality, the money market funds that are limited to Treasury securities tend to pay the lowest dividends.

Those that are diversified among corporate and governmental issuers—invested primarily in corporate IOUs called *commercial paper*—pay a bit more. Although their portfolios' credit quality may not be as high, it has to be high enough to comply with tight rules.

Two Types of Tax-Exempt Money Market Funds

Tax-exempt money market funds invest in securities of state and local governments whose interest payments, when passed through as dividends to shareholders, are exempt from federal income tax, and whose yields are lower than those of taxable securities of comparable maturities to reflect their tax-free status.

The funds are divided into two classifications: national funds with portfolios diversified among many states, and funds concentrated in securities issued by the state and local government units of single states.

Although income from both is exempt from federal income tax, the income from national funds may be subject to state (and possibly local) income tax. Income from single-state funds is likely to be double (or triple) exempt.

WHY YOU WOULD INVEST IN A MONEY MARKET FUND

There are a number of reasons why you would invest in a money market fund:

- To provide for the portion of your assets that you want to allocate to cash reserves.

- To provide a temporary parking place for a large sum of money—such as that received from your employer's retirement plan—that you intend to invest gradually in bond and/or equity funds.

-tip- **Handy for Rollovers**   A money market fund comes in handy when you have only 60 days, under Internal Revenue Service regulations, to roll over money from your employer's 401(k) plan into an IRA. You move the lump sum into the fund and then deploy it among other funds at your own pace.

- To enjoy the flexibility of a convenient income-producing savings-type account from which you can take out money—by requesting a check or by writing one yourself—without worrying about a penalty for an early withdrawal.

- To have access to the yields of money market instruments, which may exceed those of savings-type accounts and inflation, as Table 8.1 illustrates.

- To be able to earn tax-exempt income from a savings-type account.

TABLE 8.1   TAXABLE MONEY MARKET FUND YIELDS: HOW THEY COMPARE WITH BANK SAVINGS ACCOUNTS AND INFLATION 1986–1995

YEAR	MONEY MARKET FUND YIELDS	BANK SAVINGS ACCOUNT YIELDS	INFLATION
1986	6.3%	6.0%	1.1%
1987	6.1	5.4	4.4
1988	7.1	5.6	4.4
1989	8.9	6.1	4.6
1990	7.8	6.0	6.1
1991	5.7	5.2	3.1
1992	3.4	3.4	2.9
1993	2.7	2.6	2.8
1994	3.8	2.6	2.7
1995	5.5	3.1	2.5

Sources: 12-month yields on taxable money market funds, IBC's Money Fund Report; average annual yields on money market deposit and other commercial bank savings accounts, Federal Reserve System; December-to-December changes in the consumer price index, U.S. Bureau of Labor Statistics.

YOUR FIRST STEP IN CHOOSING A FUND

When choosing a money market fund, your first step is to decide whether you want to be in a taxable or a tax-exempt fund.

You want a taxable fund if:

- You are investing in a tax-deferred account, such as an IRA.

- You would have more income left after taxes than you would earn in a tax-exempt money market fund. You will need to do the calculation, based on your federal income tax bracket.

Otherwise, look at tax-exempt money market funds.

CHOOSING A MONEY MARKET FUND CATEGORY

Among taxable money market funds, your choice of a category depends largely on how you feel about credit risk.

If you would only feel comfortable in a fund that is limited to U.S. Treasury securities, you can focus your attention on that category. You must realize, though, that such a fund probably will offer a slightly lower yield than a well-diversified fund and that the Treasury won't guarantee the principal value of the fund's shares.

Otherwise, you may prefer a portfolio that is primarily invested in high-quality corporate issues and that may pay you slightly larger dividends.

Among tax-exempt funds, your choice between national and single-state funds boils down to a calculation of which would leave you with more income after taking state (and possibly local) income tax into consideration.

SELECTING A FUND THAT PROVIDES CONSISTENTLY HIGHER INCOME

Regardless of which category you choose, when you compare its leading funds to make your selection, try to find one that provides income consistently higher than that of the average fund in its group.

You'll see references to seven-day yields. Those are annualized yields, reflecting interest income for recent seven-day periods, that fund companies must calculate according to an SEC formula when they want to advertise. The standardized calculations make comparisons among funds more meaningful.

Because top funds in any category tend to choose similar securities from the same money market sectors, a major reason for differences in their yields has to be the differences in their operating expenses.

Look for a fund with low total expenses: The lower the expenses, the more a fund can pay you. When you invest in a money market fund, you shouldn't have to absorb expenses of more than 0.65% annually. Be sure to check, though, whether a fund's expenses are low because they reflect a waiver and/or reimbursement of some expenses by the fund's adviser; they could shoot up when the waiver or reimbursement ends.

! **Don't be Misled!** When a money market fund yield seems too good to be true, you may be looking at a fund whose investment adviser is temporarily waiving or reimbursing some—or even all—of its expenses. Before you invest, ask when the waiver or reimbursement will end and by how much the yield would be reduced when the expenses are imposed in full.

Differences in the average maturities of money market funds' portfolios also can result in differences in their yields.

Exercising their discretion within the 90-day average maturity that they're permitted, some portfolio managers go longer than others to lock up slightly higher yields.

What Else to Consider

If you find two or more money market funds with similar seven-day yields, performance records, and prospects, consider a few other factors in making your selection:

- *No unnecessary risks.* Read the prospectuses and shareholder reports to see whether any fund you're considering could expose you to excessively risky securities or investment techniques; ideally it should be 100% in top-quality issues, even if the SEC does permit it to be up to 5% invested in "second-tier" securities.

- *Convenience.* If the fund is part of a family of mutual funds that includes bond and equity funds in which you want to invest, switching to or from your money market fund by just calling a toll-free number would make it more convenient to manage your money.

- *Check-writing privilege.* Funds vary in the minimum amounts for which you can write checks. If you want to be able to write checks for $250, you won't want a fund with a $500 minimum.

In this lesson, you learned how to select a money market fund. In the next lesson, you learn about the different types of taxable bond funds.

9

THE DIFFERENT TYPES OF TAXABLE BOND FUNDS

In this lesson, you learn about the different types of taxable bond funds.

FUNDS FALL INTO MANY INVESTMENT OBJECTIVE CATEGORIES

On the basis of their investment objectives and policies, Lipper classifies the more than 1,500 taxable bond and income funds in existence in early 1996 into about 25 categories. Other data services and publications use fewer.

By getting a sense of how bond funds are classified, you can more easily focus your search, limiting it to funds whose investment objectives and policies most closely match your own goals and needs.

In general, Lipper classifies the funds on the basis of:

- The types of issues and issuers in which the funds invest, grouping them according to the levels of credit and other risks to which they would expose you.

Credit Risk   The risk that the issuer of a bond won't pay interest or repay principal when scheduled.

- The weighted average maturities of the securities in their portfolios, which indicate the levels of interest rate risk to which they would expose you

Interest Rate Risk   The risk that the price of a bond will fall when interest rates rise. Bond funds invested in longer-term bonds expose you to greater interest rate risk than bond funds invested in short-term bonds.

- Their linkage to the stock market, through investment in bonds (and preferred stocks) convertible into common stocks or relatively small positions in stocks themselves, thereby exposing you to stock market risk

- Their investment in foreign bonds, which expose you to currency risk

Currency Risk   The risk that the currency in which a foreign bond (or stock) is issued will decline against the U.S. dollar, causing the value of the security and its interest (or dividend) payments to fall when converted into dollars.

AN OVERVIEW OF THE U.S. INVESTMENT GRADE BOND MARKET

Before looking closely at how taxable bond funds are classified, you'll probably find it helpful to get an overview of the taxable U.S. investment grade bond market in which most of the funds are invested.

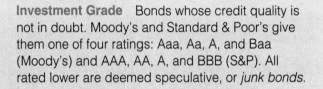

Investment Grade   Bonds whose credit quality is not in doubt. Moody's and Standard & Poor's give them one of four ratings: Aaa, Aa, A, and Baa (Moody's) and AAA, AA, A, and BBB (S&P). All rated lower are deemed speculative, or *junk bonds*.

That market is the universe of more than 5,000 fixed-rate taxable bond issues, valued at $4.5 trillion and scheduled to mature in more than one year, whose credit quality is rated by the principal rating agencies, Moody's Investors Service and Standard & Poor's, to be investment grade.

As you see in Table 9.1, U.S. Treasury securities make up almost one-half of the investment grade market. Securities backed by residential mortgages account for more than one-fourth; corporate debt, about one-sixth.

TABLE 9.1   BROAD GROUPS OF ISSUES THAT MAKE UP THE TAXABLE INVESTMENT GRADE U.S. BOND MARKET

ISSUES	SHARE OF TOTAL MARKET*
U.S. Treasury	45.06%
Federal agencies	6.62
Mortgage-backed securities	29.58

ISSUES	SHARE OF TOTAL MARKET*
Corporate	17.45
Asset-backed securities**	1.29

* As of June 1996
** Securities backed by credit card, auto, and home equity debt
Source: Aggregate Bond Index, Lehman Brothers

The sectors of the taxable investment grade bond market, on the average, had annual returns within a fairly narrow range—between 9.4% and 10.5%—over the decade ended in 1995, but in shorter periods there have been greater differences in their performance.

Corporate bonds, which usually have higher yields because of their greater average credit risk, benefited more than other sectors, on the average, during periods of falling interest rates because their average maturities tend to be longer.

GROUPING FUNDS ACCORDING TO THE ISSUES THEY INVEST IN

In dividing bond funds according to the types of issues they are primarily invested in, Lipper uses both narrow and broad classifications, some of which are further divided according to the average maturities of the funds' portfolios. The broad classes are

- *U.S. Treasury funds*, which may only invest in Treasury issues

- *U.S. government funds*, which may invest not only in Treasury issues but also in federal agency securities and in mortgage-backed securities that are guaranteed by the Government National Mortgage Association (GNMA) or issued by the Federal Home Loan Mortgage Corporation (FHLMC) or the Federal National Mortgage Association (FNMA)

- *Mortgage-backed securities funds*, which invest in securities that are guaranteed by GNMA—and thus backed by the U.S. government—or that are issued by FHLMC and FNMA, both government-created but now stockholder-owned

- *A-rated and BBB-rated corporate bond funds*, which are primarily invested in higher-quality corporate bonds—those rated A or BBB (or better)—and in government securities

- *General bond funds*, which may be invested in U.S. and/or foreign government issues and in high-, medium-, or low-quality corporates

- *High current yield funds*, which may be primarily invested in corporate bonds that are rated below investment grade

In credit risk, these groups of funds run the range from low (Treasury) to high (high yield). All but the Treasury funds also may involve call or prepayment risk.

Call or Prepayment Risk   The risk that, when interest rates decline, corporations and homeowners will call or prepay their outstanding bonds or mortgages and replace them with new ones at lower yields, reducing the income of funds that hold corporate bonds and mortgage-backed securities.

DIVIDING FUNDS ACCORDING TO MATURITIES

Lipper divides the Treasury, U.S. government, and mixed investment grade fund groups into categories according to the ranges of their portfolios' average maturities because of the impact that maturities have on fund performance. When interest rates rise, funds with the shortest average maturities drop less than those with the longest maturities. When interest rates fall, funds with the shortest maturities rise less. Lipper's maturity ranges are

- *Short*, for funds whose portfolios have weighted average maturities of less than three years

- *Short-intermediate*, one to five years

- *Intermediate*, five to ten years

Although Lipper doesn't use the phrase *long-term* in the names of categories, those whose names don't refer to other maturities either may indeed include funds with portfolios having average maturities of ten years or more.

BOND FUNDS LINKED TO THE STOCK MARKET

Bond funds may be linked to the stock market in one of two ways: by being partially invested in common stocks, as *flexible income funds* are, or by being primarily invested in bonds and preferred stocks that are convertible into common stocks. *Convertible securities funds* may have minor positions in common stocks.

Unless invested in junk bonds, such funds may have lower yields than long-term bond funds but, being linked to the stock market, they may outperform conventional bond funds when the stock market is rising.

FOREIGN BOND FUNDS INCUR ADDITIONAL RISK

Foreign bond funds are designed for investors who want a stake in overseas markets because interest rates in some countries are higher than U.S. rates at almost any time or because they expect major foreign bond markets to outperform the U.S. market.

Foreign bond funds involve essentially the same risks that domestic bond funds do and one more in addition—*currency risk*. When the dollar becomes stronger against foreign currencies, the share prices of such funds may fall.

OVER TIME, APPROPRIATE RISK-TAKING TENDS TO BE REWARDED

Study Table 9.2, and you will find that bond funds' performance, on the average, has followed the script over time, with those involving the greater interest rate risk achieving the greater returns.

TABLE 9.2 HOW TAXABLE BOND FUNDS PERFORMED IN 10-, 5-, AND 1-YEAR PERIODS ENDED IN 1995

FUND CATEGORY	AVERAGE ANNUAL TOTAL RETURNS 10 YEARS	AVERAGE ANNUAL TOTAL RETURN 5 YEARS	TOTAL RETURN 1995
Short U.S. Treasury	N/A	6.7%	11.0%
Short U.S. Government	6.8%	6.1	9.9
Short Investment Grade	7.5	6.8	9.8

Fund Category	Average Annual Total Returns 10 years	Average Annual Total Return 5 years	Total Return 1995
Short- Intermediate U.S.G.	7.6	7.2	12.5
Short- Intermediate Inv. Grade	7.6	7.6	12.8
Intermediate U.S. Treasury	7.9	8.0	15.3
Intermediate U.S. Govt.	8.6	8.0	15.7
Intermediate Investment Grade	8.6	8.9	16.5
General U.S. Treasury	10.2	10.1	22.2
General U.S. Government	8.2	8.4	17.4
Adjustable Rate Mortgage	6.8	4.9	4.7
GNMA	8.5	8.1	16.3
U.S. Mortgage	8.1	7.6	16.2
A-rated Corporate	9.2	9.7	18.5
BBB-rated Corporate	9.6	11.1	20.1
General Bond	9.1	11.9	18.0
High Current Yield	9.5	16.7	16.5
Convertible Securities	10.1	15.3	20.7
Flexible Income	9.5	10.3	16.8
Target Maturity	12.6	13.0	25.5

continues

TABLE 9.2   CONTINUED

FUND CATEGORY	AVERAGE ANNUAL TOTAL RETURNS 10 YEARS	AVERAGE ANNUAL TOTAL RETURN 5 YEARS	TOTAL RETURN 1995
Short World Multi-Market	N/A	3.9	7.9
General World Income	8.9	8.1	18.0
Emerging Markets	N/A	N/A	20.1

N/A = Not available
Source: Lipper Analytical Services

Over the decade ended in 1995, short-term funds averaged annual returns of between 7% and 7.5%; short-intermediate-term funds, around 7.5%; intermediate-term funds, between 8% and 8.5%; and long-term funds averaged more than 9%. The differences were even more pronounced in a single year, 1995, when interest rates fell and long-term funds excelled, possibly erasing memories of 1994, when just the opposite occurred.

In this lesson, you learned about the different types of bond funds. In the next lesson, you learn how to select one or more funds that meet your needs.

How to Select a Taxable Bond Fund

In this lesson, you learn how to select one or more taxable bond funds.

Start by Making a Couple of Decisions

To choose a suitable fund, you first need to decide on an investment objective. Is it maximum current income because you need the money to live on? Is it total return because you want to invest in a bond fund to reduce the risk level of a growth-oriented portfolio of equity funds?

You also need to decide how much volatility you are able and willing to accept in a fund's returns to achieve your investment objective. Can you only accept very little volatility because you will be taking your dividends in cash or because you have a fairly short investment horizon? Can you accept a higher level of volatility because you will be reinvesting your dividends, thereby buying more shares when prices are down, or because you have a long investment horizon?

THE RETURNS YOU CAN EXPECT

When you invest in a bond fund, your expected rate of return depends primarily on the level and direction of interest rates for the sector of the bond market in which the fund is invested (after taking into consideration what it costs you to buy and own the fund's shares).

Changing interest rates can have a major impact on total returns and can even cause negative total returns, as occurred in 1994.

Using data for the total taxable investment grade bond market as an example, Table 10.1 illustrates how much total returns increased and decreased from year to year as principal returns varied widely, and interest income fluctuated within a relatively narrow range—but in a generally downward trend—in the decade ended in 1995.

TABLE 10.1   RETURNS ON PRINCIPAL AND INTEREST IN THE TAXABLE INVESTMENT GRADE BOND MARKET 1986–1995

YEAR	PRINCIPAL	INTEREST	TOTAL RETURN
1986	5.2%	10.3%	15.4%
1987	−6.3	8.9	2.6
1988	−1.3	9.3	8.0
1989	4.6	9.8	14.4
1990	−0.2	9.3	9.1
1991	6.6	9.4	16.0
1992	−0.6	8.1	7.6
1993	2.3	7.6	9.9
1994	−9.6	6.8	−2.9
1995	10.4	8.1	18.5

Source: Broad Investment Grade Bond Index, Salomon Brothers.

You have no way of knowing what your absolute returns are likely to be in the years that you are invested, but you can assume that the relationship between returns for longer- and shorter-term bonds will remain unchanged. Most of the time, the rates on longer-term bonds, which involve more interest rate risk, will be higher than the rates on shorter-term bonds.

How much higher long-term yields are depends primarily on inflation expectations and the response to them by investors and the Federal Reserve.

Your Assumption of Interest Rate Risk

Whether you are investing for maximum current income or total return, you are likely to do better in a longer-term bond fund than in a shorter-term fund. However, because the longer-term fund would expose you to more interest rate risk, it is critical for you to consider how much risk you are able and willing to accept.

When interest rates rise, the full faith and credit of the U.S. doesn't keep the prices of Treasury issues from falling along with the rest of the market.

How much interest rate risk you can accept depends on

- Whether you will take the dividends in cash (thereby depriving yourself of the opportunity to pick up additional shares at lower prices by reinvesting them)

- How long you plan to be invested

CHOOSING A FUND ON THE BASIS OF ITS INTEREST RATE RISK LEVEL

You can view a bond fund's level of interest rate risk in terms of the weighted average maturity of its bond portfolio, not only the current average but also the maturity range within which the adviser is permitted to manage the portfolio.

Although the SEC requires funds to state investment policies up front in their prospectuses, it does not require them to refer to the maturity range in their names. If, however, a name does contain such a reference, you should be able to rely on it.

What's In a Name? The SEC doesn't tell a fund company what it may call a fund, but if a fund's name indicates a bond fund's portfolio has, say, a short- or long-term average maturity, the SEC checks whether the fund is being managed accordingly.

Lipper's classification system and publications that use it provide additional help. Whatever category of funds you want to study, you can easily find a list in a reference source such as *Standard & Poor's/Lipper Mutual Fund ProFiles*, a quarterly, or identify the funds in the tables published every Friday by *The Wall Street Journal*.

SOME RULES OF THUMB TO GUIDE YOU

To aid you in culling for your review funds whose interest rate risk levels match your risk tolerance level, there are some rules of thumb. One approach is simply to confine your search to short-term funds, if you only can tolerate a little volatility;

long-term funds if you can tolerate a greater degree of volatility; or short-intermediate or intermediate funds, if you are somewhere in between.

Other strategies involve what is known as a fund's *duration*, which you may be able to get from a fund company by phone, if you don't find it in the fund's literature, or from a reference work in your library.

 Duration   A measure of a bond's or bond fund's sensitivity to changes in interest rates, based on a complicated calculation that takes into consideration, among other things, the cash flows of interest payments and principal repayments.

Expressed in years, duration is the most meaningful measure of a bond's or bond fund's sensitivity to changes in interest rates. A bond with a duration of two years will go up or down about 2% if interest rates go down or up 1%; a bond with a duration of five years will go up or down 5%, and so on. If, for example, you have an investment horizon of three years, you would only want to be in short-term funds, which usually would have a duration of less than two years.

If your investment horizon is ten years or longer, you might be able to accept a fund with a duration of eight to ten years.

Intermediate-term funds tend to have durations of four to five years.

GO FOR THE LEADERS

After you have made a list of funds in the category that you've targeted, compare their performance to determine the leaders from which you will choose one.

Because performance in any single period—especially a brief
one—is not meaningful, compare the total returns of the
funds for various periods, such as one, five, and ten years, to
determine which one(s) consistently outperformed the average
returns for the group. If a fund has been in operation for five
years or less, look at returns for three years.

Having narrowed the group down to a few attractive candidates, see how their performance compares with benchmark
indexes of the total taxable investment grade bond market,
such as Lehman Brothers' Aggregate Index or Salomon Brothers' Broad Investment Grade Index, or a relevant index of the
market sector in which the funds are primarily invested.

Because such indexes constitute tougher standards than averages for peer fund groups—which are weighed down by the
returns of poorly managed funds—the SEC requires fund
managements to pick the "appropriate" benchmark indexes
that their funds are to be compared with and to provide
comparative return data in fund literature.

Remember that indexes, unlike bond funds, reflect no annual
expenses. A fund that approximates or beats its benchmark
index and significantly beats its competitors over several
periods has to impress you.

LOOKING AT YIELDS

Yields should not be the sole reason you choose a bond fund,
but they obviously are a significant factor, especially if you are
investing for current income.

The fund yield that you want to know is not, however, the
widely publicized 12-month yield, which is calculated by dividing the total of a fund's income dividend distributions over
12 months by its NAV at the end of the 12-month period.

This historic figure, more properly called the *distribution rate*, can be misleading when you are considering what to invest in for the future. It can be higher or lower than a fund's yield is now, depending on what happened to interest rates over the 12 months.

A more meaningful yield figure is the annualized rate for the latest 30-day period that the SEC requires bond funds to use for advertising and other promotional purposes. It is more meaningful not just because it is more current.

What makes it important is that, in calculating it according to a standard formula that the SEC imposes, a fund company has to take two major factors into consideration:

- *Loads.* If a fund charges a front-end sales load, it has to be factored in. Thus, if a no-load fund and a load fund are identical in every other aspect, the no-load fund will have a higher 30-day yield.

- *Bond premiums and discounts.* It's common for some bonds in a portfolio to be trading at a premium and for others to be trading at a discount. By the time they mature, the prices of both types will have to fall or rise to their face values.

The latter factor should help to prevent you from unintentionally falling for a high-yielding fund whose portfolio is stuffed with bonds selling at premiums that will evaporate over time, as the bonds approach maturity dates, and thus lead to erosion of principal.

In this lesson, you learned how to select a suitable taxable bond fund. In the next lesson, you learn about tax-exempt bond funds.

THE DIFFERENT TYPES OF TAX-EXEMPT BOND FUNDS

In this lesson, you learn about the different types of tax-exempt bond funds.

WHAT IS A TAX-EXEMPT FUND?

Tax-exempt (or municipal) bond funds invest in the securities of the many state and local government units whose interest payments are not subject to federal income tax. Although commonly called *municipal bonds*, tax-exempt securities are actually issued by various levels of state and local governments.

Consider these types of funds only if they would provide you more income than a taxable bond fund, with similar risk and reward characteristics, after you deduct the federal, state, and possibly local income taxes that you would owe on any distribution of income dividends. Otherwise, it would make no sense. Tax-exempt securities pay lower yields than taxable securities of comparable interest rate risk and credit quality to reflect the tax exemption.

KNOWING WHEN TO CONSIDER THEM

There are essentially two ways to calculate whether you should consider tax-exempt securities:

1. Take the yield of a taxable bond fund, subtract the federal and state (and any local) income tax that you would owe on it, and see whether the after-tax yield is exceeded by the yield of a comparable tax-exempt fund—that is, one with a comparable duration and similar credit quality.

2. Take the yield of a tax-exempt fund and calculate its taxable equivalent yield. If, say, you consider a tax-exempt fund with a 5% yield and you are in the 28% federal income tax bracket, convert the 28% to a decimal, 0.28; subtract that from 1.00, and you get 0.72. Divide the 5.00 by 0.72, and you get 6.94. Thus, 6.94% is the taxable equivalent yield for a tax-exempt 5% security. If you can find a taxable bond fund of comparable risk that yields more than 6.94%, you would be better off investing in it and paying the taxes. For other scenarios, see Table 11.1.

TABLE 11.1 TAXABLE EQUIVALENT YIELD TABLE

TAX BRACKET	TAXABLE EQUIVALENT RATES BASED ON TAX-EXEMPT FEDERAL INCOME YIELD OF					
	2%	**3%**	**4%**	**5%**	**6%**	**7%**
15%	2.35%	3.53%	4.71%	5.88%	7.06%	8.24%
28%	2.78	4.17	5.56	6.94	8.33	9.72
31%	2.90	4.35	5.80	7.25	8.70	10.14
36%	3.13	4.69	6.25	7.81	9.38	10.94
39.6%	3.31	4.97	6.62	8.28	9.93	11.59

Source: Vanguard Municipal Bond Fund Prospectus, December 29, 1995.

Equivalent Taxable Yield   The yield a taxable fund has to exceed to make it more attractive than the yield of a comparable tax-exempt fund that you're considering.

IMPORTANT POINTS TO REMEMBER

When you're considering tax-exempt funds, remember the following important points:

- Tax-exempt funds are not always totally tax-free. When a fund realizes net short-term and/or long-term capital gains and has to distribute them to shareholders, they are as taxable as the capital gains distributions of taxable bond funds.

- Even income distributions are not always tax-free. If they reflect tax-exempt interest earned on certain *private activity* bonds—as defined by the tax law— they may constitute what are called *tax preference items*. If you're subject to the federal alternative minimum tax (AMT), you may be subject to taxes.

WHAT TAX-EXEMPT BOND FUNDS INVEST IN

To provide investors tax-exempt income, municipal bond funds invest in two types of securities:

- *General obligation issues* whose interest payment and principal repayment obligations may be supported by tax revenues collected by the state and local governments that sold them.

- *Revenue bonds* whose debt service has to be supported by receipts from user fees and other sources that are collected by the turnpike authorities, water districts, and other units that sold them. Because such fees often depend on economic conditions, some of these securities are more speculative investments than others.

Funds tend to be more heavily invested in revenue bonds because, on the average, they tend to provide higher returns.

These Bonds also Vary in Credit Quality

Like taxable corporate bonds, tax-exempt bonds vary in credit quality and are commonly rated by rating agencies. While some are also rated triple-A, defaults tend to be less frequent. Some issues are so small that their issuers don't want to go to the expense of obtaining ratings.

A large number of state and local government units take out insurance policies from municipal bond insurance companies to assure investors that interest and principal will be paid when scheduled. They are likely to do so when the coverage helps them to sell their bonds.

 Insured Municipal Bonds Municipal bonds covered by bond insurance. The insurance guarantees timely payment of interest and repayment of principal to bond holders, such as mutual funds. It does not guarantee the funds' share prices!

Bonds covered by top-rated insurance companies are endowed with their credit quality. If a company issuing a policy is rated triple-A, the municipal bonds that it insures are likely to be rated triple-A, too.

NATIONAL VERSUS SINGLE-STATE FUNDS

Tax-exempt bond funds are divided into two broad groups:

- *National funds,* which are usually invested in the securities of a large number of state and local government units. Their income dividends may be subject to your state (and local) income tax.

- *Single-state funds,* which are concentrated in securities issued within one state. To mitigate credit risk, they may be significantly invested in insured municipal bonds. Income from such funds is usually exempt from state (and local) income tax for residents of the states in which they are concentrated.

A CHOICE OF MATURITIES

As classified by Lipper, tax-exempt bond funds fall into four maturity groupings:

- *Short-term,* for funds whose portfolios have weighted average maturities of three years or less

- *Short-intermediate-term,* one to five years

- *Intermediate-term,* five to ten years

- *Long-term,* for funds divided into three categories— *general, insured,* and *high yield*—and that tend to have portfolios with average maturities of ten years or more

As with taxable bond funds, the tax-exempt bond funds with the longest average maturities (or durations) fall more when interest rates rise and rise more when interest rates fall.

Municipal bond funds may involve call risk, as corporate bond funds do. That is, when interest rates fall, issuers of their securities may have the right to call them before they mature and replace them, in accordance with the bonds' provisions, to reduce their borrowing costs.

Classifying Funds According to Credit Quality

Both national and single-state funds are also classified according to credit quality.

As noted above, Lipper uses three categories:

- *General*, for funds primarily invested in bonds of investment grade.

- *Insured*, for funds primarily invested in bonds insured when they were bought or for which the funds purchased insurance after acquiring them.

- *High yield*, for funds invested in higher-yielding muni bonds. They may include bonds rated below investment grade but are not primarily invested in muni junk.

In this lesson, you learned about the various types of tax-exempt bond funds that are available. In the next lesson, you learn how to select the best tax-exempt bond fund for your portfolio.

How to Select a Tax-Exempt Bond Fund

In this lesson, you learn how to select one or more tax-exempt bond funds.

Identifying the Right Tax-Exempt Bond Fund

As with taxable bond funds, you don't pick a tax-exempt fund by simply finding the one with the highest yield.

You should identify a leading fund in an appropriate category whose investment objectives, policies, and risk characteristics are compatible with your goals, investment horizon, and risk tolerance.

Choosing a Category

It's easier to choose a category in the universe of tax-exempt funds because there aren't as many.

To do so, you have to make only three decisions:

- Nationally diversified funds or single-state funds

- Funds with greater interest rate risk or those with less risk

- Funds with low credit risk or those with moderate risk

National versus Single-State Funds

The choice between national and single-state funds depends on the variety of single-state funds available in your state, your analysis as to which one would give you more income, and your feelings about your state's economic prospects.

> **tip**
>
> **State Pride** Though admirable, pride in your state should have nothing to do with whether you choose a single-state fund that's available to you. The choice of such fund should be based on what is most appropriate for you from an investment standpoint.

While the selections of single-state funds in many states have become diverse, your state may only have a limited number of single-state funds. In that case, you may have to pick a national fund.

But assuming that you have the opportunity to choose, which would provide you with more income?

Compare the yields of both types of funds with similar investment objectives and risk characteristics and see whether the single-state funds would pay you more than you would have left from a national fund after paying state (and local) income taxes.

As for economic prospects, if, for example, you are concerned about the levels of tax receipts supporting general obligation bonds—or of revenues that support revenue bonds—you might opt for a nationally diversified fund, unless a single-state fund invested in insured municipal bonds is available.

INTEREST RATE RISK IS CRUCIAL

Whether you invest in a national or a single-state fund, the interest rate risk of the fund is crucial:

- If you plan to invest in a tax-exempt fund for income—and, therefore, won't be reinvesting dividends—or if you are planning to stay in such a fund for only a few years, you should focus on funds in the short-term category.

- If you plan to invest for total return, reinvest dividends, and stay in a fund for ten years or more, you may consider any of the three long-term categories: general, insured, or high yield.

- If your investment horizon is somewhere in-between, the short-intermediate or intermediate category should give you the opportunity to find a fund that reconciles your return target with your risk tolerance in way acceptable to you.

FUNDS VARY IN CREDIT QUALITY, TOO

Although the world of tax-exempt bond funds does not offer the wide range in credit quality that you find in the taxable bond fund market, it does offer a quality range.

If you're most comfortable with funds invested in securities of the highest credit quality, you may want to limit your research to those in the insured category—especially if you're planning to invest in a single-state fund.

If you are more relaxed about credit quality, general municipal bond funds would be the ones to study. If you are very relaxed about credit quality, you may want at least to have a look at high-yield funds.

The Returns You Can Expect

Funds that involve less risk are likely to provide lower returns, and funds that involve more risk are likely—but not guaranteed—to provide higher returns over time.

As Table 12.1 indicates, the average maturity of tax-exempt funds, which reflects your probable exposure to interest rate risk, was a far more important determinant of returns in the decade ended in 1995 than credit quality.

Table 12.1 How Tax-Exempt Bond Funds Have Performed—and How They've Compared with Their Benchmarks in 10-, 5-, and 1-Year Periods Ended in 1995

Bond Fund Category/ Bond Market Sector	Average Annual Total Return 10 Years	Average Annual Total Return 5 Years	Total Return 1995
Short-Term Municipal Funds	5.5%	5.1%	6.9%
Short-Intermediate-Term Funds	6.4	6.3	8.3
Intermediate-Term Funds	7.6	7.4	12.9
General Municipal Funds	8.6	8.5	16.8
Insured Municipal Funds	8.3	8.3	17.6

continues

TABLE 12.1   CONTINUED

BOND FUND CATEGORY/ BOND MARKET SECTOR	AVERAGE ANNUAL TOTAL RETURN 10 YEARS	AVERAGE ANNUAL TOTAL RETURN 5 YEARS	TOTAL RETURN 1995
High Yield Municipal Funds	8.5	8.4	16.0
5-Year Municipal Bond Index	N/A	7.5	11.7
10-Year Municipal Bond Index	9.2	9.0	17.2
Long Municipal Bond Index	10.3	10.0	23.3

N/A = Not available

Sources: Lehman Brothers Municipal Bond Index, Lipper Analytical Services

As if following a script that you could have written easily, short-intermediate-term funds outperformed short-term funds, on the average, and were themselves outperformed by inter-mediate-term funds. The three long-term categories, in turn, outperformed intermediate-term funds; it seemed to matter little whether the funds were concentrated in insured bonds, high-yield bonds, or a cross-section of investment grade bonds.

GO FOR THE LEADERS

As with taxable bond funds, after you have chosen the cat-egory of funds in which you want to invest, cull out for evalu-ation funds whose total returns have consistently made them their group's leading performers for one-, five-, and ten-year periods.

You also may want to look at three-year performance—especially if too few prospects have been in operation for more than five years.

Next, compare the total returns over these periods with an appropriate benchmark index, such as one of those calculated by Lehman Brothers, to narrow your list down to those that beat the index or came closest to matching it. Don't expect to find many that beat the index. Be glad if you find a few that came within, say, 0.5% of annual average index returns—or roughly the margin accounted for by reasonable fund expenses.

Look at Yields

To help you to identify the most promising funds in your sample, compare their 30-day SEC-basis yields, which you should be able to get easily from the fund companies.

These standardized yields reflect not only the interest income earned by funds but also the sales charges (if any) and the amortization of premiums for bonds selling above face value and of discounts for bonds selling below.

High yields do not necessarily mean that funds are well managed, and low yields do not necessarily mean that funds involve high costs—although they often do.

A high yield could mean that a fund's investment adviser has been temporarily waiving or reimbursing some expenses, while a low yield could reflect a fund's concentration in higher quality or shorter-maturity securities.

In this lesson, you learned how to select a tax-exempt bond fund. In the next lesson, you learn about the different types of equity funds.

THE DIFFERENT TYPES OF EQUITY FUNDS

In this lesson, you learn about the different types of equity (or common stock) funds.

WHAT YOU SHOULD KNOW ABOUT COMMON STOCKS

The frequent references to "the stock market" that you hear could lead you to think that the securities that are traded, representing interests in the profits and dividends of thousands of corporations, are homogeneous. In fact, all stocks are not the same because all companies are not alike. All common stocks don't have the same potential for risk and reward. Among other things, stocks vary according to

- The financial strength of the corporations that issued them

- The industries or economic sectors in which their issuers do business

- The countries in which they operate

- The growth rates of the companies' revenues and earnings

- Their dividends' yields

- The ratios of their prices to variables such as earnings or book value per share

- The sizes of the companies' capitalizations, or "caps"

It may be easy to see why the growth rate of a company's earnings, the yield on its stock, and the relationship of its share price to earnings per share are important, but the importance of other variables, such as book value per share or a company's capitalization, may not be self-evident.

Book value, which reflects the historic cost of a company's assets less the outstanding debts, is an important tool for analysts who want to determine whether a stock is cheap or expensive. When the market value of a company's stock is a lot higher than its book value, some money managers may pass it up in the belief that the stock is overpriced. When the market value is lower, some may snap up the stock in the belief that it's a bargain. Both groups could be wrong.

Capitalization is commonly used by money managers who choose stocks on the basis of company size.

Book Value Per Share   The total of a company's assets less its liabilities, divided by the number of its shares of common stock.

Capitalization   The value of one share of a company's stock times the number of shares outstanding. A company whose shares are worth $10 each and which has ten million shares outstanding has a "cap" of $100 million.

WHAT INVESTMENT ADVISERS EMPHASIZE WHEN PICKING STOCKS

The investment advisers who manage equity funds consider these and other factors when they select stocks for fund port-folios, giving higher or lower weight to each as required or preferred to comply with their funds' investment objectives and policies.

Pursuing fund objectives and policies as well as their own in-vestment styles, advisers may focus on sectors of the stock market, such as the following:

- *Value stocks*, those that sell at low multiples of com-panies' earnings or book values per share.

- *Growth stocks*, those of companies whose sales and earnings are rising at above-average rates. The prices of such stocks may be high in relation to earnings or book values.

- *Large-cap stocks*, those of companies with large capi-talizations. Such stocks may fall less if the market drops.

- *Small-cap stocks*, those of companies with small capi-talizations. Definitions of "small" vary widely, with the top of the range running as high as $750 million or even higher. Small-cap stocks have outperformed large-cap stocks, on the average, over long periods of time. They also are more volatile.

- *Mid-cap stocks*, those of companies whose capitaliza-tions are in-between small and large.

HOW THEIR RETURNS COMPARE

Table 13.1 gives you a sense of how stocks in different sectors of the U.S. stock market have performed in comparison with one another and with the broad market, as measured by some of the popular indexes calculated by Frank Russell Company, Standard & Poor's Corporation (S&P), and Wilshire Associates Incorporated.

Whether you're looking at the S&P 500, the Russell 1000, the Russell 3000, or the Wilshire 5000, you see that average annual returns were around 14.5% and 16.5% to 17%, respectively, for the ten and five years ended in 1995.

(The S&P 500 accounts for about 70% of the market cap of all the stocks traded in the U.S.; the Russell 3000, 98%; and the Wilshire 5000, essentially 100% of all 6,800 U.S.-headquartered companies.)

TABLE 13.1 HOW THE STOCK MARKET AND ITS SECTORS PERFORMED IN 10-, 5-, AND 1-YEAR PERIODS ENDED IN 1995

MARKET SECTOR	AVERAGE ANNUAL TOTAL RETURN 10 YEARS	AVERAGE ANNUAL TOTAL RETURN 5 YEARS	TOTAL RETURN 1995
Standard & Poor's 500 Index	14.5%	16.6%	37.6%
S&P 500/BARRA Value	14.7	16.9	37.0
S&P 500/BARRA Growth	14.7	16.1	38.1
Russell 1000 Index	14.7	17.2	37.8
Russell 1000 Value	14.5	17.8	38.4
Russell 1000 Growth	14.7	16.5	37.2

continues

TABLE 13.1   CONTINUED

MARKET SECTOR	AVERAGE ANNUAL TOTAL RETURN 10 YEARS	AVERAGE ANNUAL TOTAL RETURN 5 YEARS	TOTAL RETURN 1995
Russell Mid-cap	14.7	19.9	34.5
Russell 2000	11.3	21.0	28.4
Russell 2000 Value	12.3	22.9	25.8
Russell 2000 Growth	10.1	18.8	31.0
Russell 3000	14.4	17.4	36.8
Russell 3000 Growth	14.3	16.6	36.6
Russell 3000 Value	14.3	18.1	37.0
Wilshire 5000	14.2	17.3	36.5

Sources: Frank Russell Company, Standard & Poor's Corporation, Wilshire Associates Incorporated.

Large-Cap   The 500 companies that make up the Standard & Poor's 500 Index had an average market capitalization of $9.2 billion at the end of 1995. Three of them—GE, AT&T, and Exxon—had market caps of $100 billion or more. Coca-Cola wasn't far behind. They and only 54 other companies account for one-half of the total cap of all 500.

Although value stocks excelled in some periods and growth stocks excelled in others, the table shows that there was not much difference, on the average, in their performance over the decade.

Table 13.1 also shows that small-cap stocks, as measured by the Russell 2000, do not always beat large-cap stocks. There have been periods, which have lasted as long as a few years, when they have lagged.

HOW EQUITY FUNDS ARE CLASSIFIED

Whether limited to stocks in accordance with certain "cap" preferences and investment styles, such as small-cap value or large-cap growth, or invested in widely diversified portfolios, the more than 2,000 equity funds in operation vary considerably in their investment objectives and policies.

To find one or more funds suitable for you, it helps if you understand what fund and data companies consider in classifying them.

Lipper's fine-tuning results in the largest number of investment objective categories—around 30. They are used widely in fund companies' literature and in publications that you may read.

As a first cut, Lipper essentially assigns all equity funds to three broad groupings:

- *General equity funds*, those invested in widely diversified portfolios of stocks

- *Sector funds*, those concentrated in stocks of companies within a single industry or economic sector

- *Foreign stock funds*, those heavily, if not primarily, invested in stocks of foreign corporations

As a general rule, you may consider sector and foreign stock funds more risky than general equity funds—sector funds, because of their concentration; foreign stock funds, because of their exposure to exchange rate fluctuations and other risks associated with investing in other countries.

CHARACTERIZING THE CATEGORIES

Lipper divides general equity funds into seven categories. Of these, five have no targeted ranges of capitalizations. Four of them may include funds with different mixes of large-, medium-, and/or small-cap stocks.

- *Capital appreciation funds*, Lipper's most aggressive category, involve high portfolio turnover rates—with associated transaction costs and (taxable) capital gains distributions for their shareholders.

- *Growth stock funds*, the most popular equity fund category, invest in stocks of companies expected to enjoy above-average earnings growth—but their managers aren't as likely to pursue more aggressive portfolio management techniques.

- *Growth & income funds*, the second most popular category, emphasize growth, as the name suggests, but also are managed to generate relatively high—or growing—income dividends. They may tend to be heavily invested in value stocks.

- *Equity-income funds* are similar to growth & income funds but tend to give more emphasis to income and less to growth.

- *S&P 500 funds*—funds that are managed to match the performance of the S&P 500 Index—were in the growth & income category until Lipper broke them out when the group became large. Because the index is considered a large-cap index, the category comes closest to being a category for funds concentrated in large-cap stocks, although the index does include smaller and medium-sized companies in industries that lack giants.

- The *mid-cap* and *small company growth fund* categories are the only two whose funds are classified by Lipper according to cap size. The categories' funds tend to be more volatile than large-cap funds.

Both sector funds and foreign stock funds are likely to incur more stock market risk than general equity funds, but some are more risky than others.

In line with SEC requirements that a fund's investment practices must be consistent with a fund's name, sector funds must be at least 65% invested in the industries in which they are concentrated; some may be 80% or more invested in them. The rest of the funds' portfolios may be in other industries and/or cash to moderate risk.

Utility funds may be the least volatile of these. Other sector classifications used by Lipper are science & technology, health/biotechnology, financial services, gold, natural resources, real estate, and environmental.

Foreign stock funds are primarily classified on the basis of their geographical mixes. Both international and global funds are invested in diversified portfolios of foreign stocks; the difference between them is that global funds also may be invested in U.S. stocks.

A minority of foreign stock funds are concentrated in the Pacific region, Europe, Canada, Latin America, and emerging markets generally.

In this lesson, you learned about the different types of equity funds. In the next lesson, you learn how to select one or more equity funds that match your investment objectives.

HOW TO SELECT ONE OR MORE EQUITY FUNDS

In this lesson, you learn how to select one or more equity funds that match your investment objectives.

WHAT TO LOOK FOR IN AN EQUITY FUND

If you expect to rely heavily on equity funds to help you accumulate a retirement nest egg or meet another important goal, make your choice carefully and deliberately. Take the time to do at least four things:

- Decide what you want to achieve: capital appreciation, income, or both?

- Think hard about how many years you plan to be invested. Do you have at least five to ten years in mind?

> ! **Avoid Short-Term Investing** If you only plan to be invested a few years—say, three years or fewer—buying an equity fund could be unwise. The stock market could enter a down phase soon after you buy and not recover fully by the time you need the money.

- Reflect on how much short-term volatility you are able and willing to accept. Are you sure that you won't lose sleep if the stock market drops, say, 10% during the period that you own equity funds? How about 20%?

- Consider an investment strategy that involves assembling a portfolio of several funds.

One Equity Fund or More

If an equity mutual fund is diversified among a large number of common stocks to reduce investment risk, why should you think about owning a portfolio that's diversified among several equity funds?

Because stock market leadership tends to rotate among sectors and investment styles.

It's prudent, therefore, to plan on having a portfolio of funds of different types, blended in proportions appropriate to your goals and risk tolerance.

If you only have—and expect to have—enough money to invest in one fund, don't hesitate to do so, provided that an equity fund is appropriate for you. You still would be better off than if you would risk the same amount of money in an individual company's common stock.

Your First—or Only—Equity Fund

Whether it's going to be the core of your fund portfolio or your total portfolio, your first or only equity fund should satisfy your basic investment objective and risk criteria. If you'll be investing in additional equity funds, they can provide you exposure to other investment objectives and the higher—or lower—risk levels associated with them.

For any investor—young or old, wealthy or not, working or retired—the core or only equity fund should be a general (or widely diversified) equity fund.

For many people, the growth & income category is the most appropriate first choice among general equity funds. It may be the most appropriate for you, too, because a well-managed growth & income fund should provide you:

- The prospect of appreciation close to that of the U.S. stock market as a whole

- Less volatility than a more aggressive fund that is managed to seek—but may not achieve—above-average appreciation

- A modest stream of income dividends

Such a fund probably will be fully invested—that is, 95% or more—in common stocks with the remaining 5% or less being invested in cash equivalents to provide a reserve for redemption requests. Most of its stocks are likely to pay dividends, although the fund's manager may have chosen some that don't because of their prospects for appreciation. Some growth & income funds have less in common stocks and are partially invested in convertible or nonconvertible bonds to boost their dividends.

As Table 14.1 shows, growth & income funds, on the average, have performed over time nearly as well as the Standard & Poor's 500 Index after their annual operating expenses are taken into account. Quite a few have outperformed the index.

Table 14.1 How General Equity Funds Performed—and How They've Compared with Their Benchmarks in the 10-, 5-, and 1-Year Periods Ended in 1995

Equity Fund Category/ Stock Market Sector	Average Annual Total Return 10 Years	Average Annual Total Return 5 Years	Total Return 1995
Capital Appreciation Funds	13.2%	17.7%	30.3%
Growth Funds	13.4	16.4	30.8
Mid-Cap Funds	14.4	20.0	32.2
Small Company Growth Funds	14.0	21.2	31.6
Growth & Income Funds	12.8	15.5	30.8
S&P 500 Index Funds	13.9	16.0	36.8
Equity Income Funds	12.0	15.2	30.2
General Equity Funds Average	13.2	17.0	31.1
Standard & Poor's 500 Index	14.5	16.6	37.6
Russell Mid-cap Index	14.7	19.9	34.5
Russell 2000 Index	11.3	21.0	28.4
Wilshire 5000 Index	14.2	17.3	36.5

Sources: Lipper Analytical Services, Frank Russell Company, Standard & Poor's Corporation, Wilshire Associates Incorporated.

A fund that's managed to match the S&P 500 would be an appropriate alternative (or complement) to an actively managed growth & income fund in that it also should provide growth as well as some income. You know that it will never outperform the index, and that, if properly managed, it should never lag the index by more than the fund's annual operating expenses.

You also know that it would go down when the stock market goes down; its manager would not have the flexibility to reduce his equity allocation.

CHOOSING THE FIRST FUND

By deciding to make a no-load growth & income fund your first fund, you would hold down considerably the number of general equity funds from which you need to make your selection and, thus, would simplify your task.

To choose the fund yourself, make a list of a half dozen or so leading no-load growth & income funds on which to get literature for study and comparison.

Choosing an S&P 500 Index fund is a lot easier. All you really need to do is pick one whose total returns come closest to the index because of the way it's managed and because of its low expenses, as epitomized by the oldest and largest such fund, Vanguard Index Trust's 500 Portfolio (whose annual expenses are a mere 0.2%).

How do you make up a list of leading actively managed growth & income funds for your study? Go to your library's personal finance shelf, find a comprehensive reference work on mutual funds that contains performance data calculated by Lipper or another reputable firm, and turn to the section listing growth & income funds. If you can only get your hands on a source whose data are organized by fund companies, instead of by categories, you'll have to run down the list to cull out those labeled as being in the growth & income category (or any other category that you're looking for).

Look for no-load growth & income funds whose total returns have consistently exceeded both those of the average of their category, as calculated by Lipper or another firm, and those of the S&P 500 Index for the last one-, five-, and ten-year periods.

If you find a half dozen or so, consider your first step a success and dial the funds' 800 numbers (which you should find in the same reference source) to order copies of the current prospectuses and most recent annual or semiannual reports to shareholders. If you only can find funds that have beaten the benchmarks in two of three periods, order literature from those.

CHOOSING A MORE AGGRESSIVE GENERAL EQUITY FUND

If you also want to invest in one or more aggressive general equity funds because you expect such funds to provide even higher returns, you can look for it (them) in categories called *aggressive growth* (or capital appreciation, in Lipper's case) or *growth*.

Whether invested in large-, mid-, and/or small-cap stocks, funds in these categories tend to emphasize capital appreciation and give little or no importance to income. The managers of some may turn over their portfolios frequently, generating capital gains (if they do so successfully) that have to be distributed to shareholders and become taxable to you, if you own the funds in taxable accounts.

In addition or instead, you may want to find a fund concentrated in mid- or small-cap stocks because funds in these classifications have significantly outperformed large-cap funds over some periods.

Whichever you choose to look into, remember that funds in the mid- and small-cap categories tend to be more volatile than growth & income, equity income, or S&P 500 Index funds. While some reference sources break out small- and/or mid-cap funds, others combine one or both of these fund categories with aggressive growth and/or growth funds.

As in the case of growth & income funds, you would comb through the categories you're focusing on to identify a half dozen or so no-load funds that have outperformed their peers over various periods of time.

SOURCES OF MUTUAL FUND PERFORMANCE DATA

Reference sources that provide comprehensive mutual fund performance data fall into three groups: those that have organized information by fund categories (such as growth & income); those that have organized it alphabetically by funds (and indicate each fund's category); and those that offer some data by categories and some by funds.

Those providing information both ways include *Standard & Poor's/ Lipper Mutual Fund ProFiles*, *Morningstar Mutual Funds*, *The Value Line Mutual Fund Survey*, *The Individual Investor's Guide to Low-Load Mutual Funds* (published by The American Association of Individual Investors), and *The Handbook For No-Load Fund Investors* (by The No-Load Fund Investor, Inc., publisher of a monthly newsletter).

Those providing information only by fund categories include the *Investor's Guide to Low-Cost Mutual Funds* (published by Mutual Fund Education Alliance).

Those providing information by funds include *Barron's*, *The Wall Street Journal*, and *CDA/Wiesenberger Mutual Funds Report*.

In addition, some magazines provide fund performance data in different ways at different intervals. They include *Business Week*, *Consumer Reports*, *Forbes*, *Money*, and *Kiplinger's Personal Finance Magazine*.

Publications that list funds by categories but don't provide individual funds' performance data include the *Directory of Mutual Funds*, a comprehensive guide to funds sponsored by members of the Investment Company Institute, and the *100% No-Load Mutual Fund Investment Guide and Member Fund Directory*, a guide to the funds sponsored by the few dozen companies belonging to the 100% No-Load Mutual Fund Council. You can use either of these to get the names of funds in various categories and then look up their performance data elsewhere.

Although it may be convenient to use these sources in your favorite library, you may find it even more convenient to have them at home by buying or subscribing to those that you find useful, if you expect to invest enough money to make it worthwhile.

In addition to, or instead of, also comparing the funds' performance with that of the S&P 500 Index, which reflects the performance of both growth and value large-cap stocks, it probably would be more meaningful to compare their total returns with those of more relevant growth stock indexes. In the case of large-cap growth funds, that could be the S&P/BARRA or Russell 1000 Growth Index, for example; in the case of small- or mid-cap growth funds, the appropriate Russell 2000 or Mid-Cap Growth Index.

> **Finding a Benchmark**   Instead of wondering which benchmark index would be appropriate for funds in a given category, you may find a clue in their pamphlets, as fund companies are required to choose relevant benchmarks for comparisons in their literature.

Investing in Sector or Foreign Stock Funds

After developing the nucleus of a portfolio of equity funds, you may be tempted to consider adding a bit of spice in the form of sector and foreign stock funds. Think carefully about whether either would be suitable for you.

Sector Funds

Sector funds' performance has ranged widely. In the five years ended in 1995, for example, funds concentrated in financial services and science and technology stocks had total returns averaging around 28%, whereas gold and environmental funds returned only around 5%. In 1995—an extraordinary year for common stocks, to be sure—gold funds returned less than 2%, which was less than money market funds.

Clearly, sector funds are not for everyone and, in many—if not most—cases, are not meant to be investments that you just buy and hold.

FOREIGN STOCK FUNDS

A stronger argument can be made for investing in a fund that owns a diversified portfolio of foreign stocks, but it may not be sufficient to persuade you to buy one.

The argument for investing abroad is not only that a foreign stock fund might moderate the volatility of a domestic stock fund portfolio, but also that there have been—and may again be—periods in which foreign stock markets outperform the U.S. stock market.

The trouble with that argument is that it isn't enough for U.S. investors that foreign stock markets excel in local currencies; their returns also have to excel when translated into U.S. dollars.

In the decade ended in 1995, stock markets in the major industrial countries, as measured by the Morgan Stanley Capital International Europe, Australia, and Far East (EAFE) Index, have not done as well as the U.S. market.

If you want to have a stake in foreign markets, consider a superior, widely diversified international fund that beats the EAFE Index (in U.S. dollars) as well as the average of its peers. Funds concentrated in regions of the world or in emerging markets tend to be more risky and don't always provide higher returns.

In this lesson, you learned how to select one or more equity funds that match your investment needs. In the next lesson, you learn about the various types of mixed assets funds.

15

HOW TO SELECT
A SUITABLE
MIXED ASSETS FUND

In this lesson, you learn how to select a suitable mixed assets fund.

THE DIFFERENT TYPES OF MIXED ASSETS FUNDS

Lipper has classified such funds into five categories: balanced, flexible portfolio, global flexible portfolio, income, and flexible income. The flexible portfolio category includes funds known as *asset allocation funds*, for which other data firms use a separate category.

Whatever they're called, the asset mixes of mixed assets funds and their securities selection policies vary considerably, depending on the funds' investment objectives and the weight given to each:

- Maximum total return consistent with moderate risk

- Income

- Preservation of principal

Balanced funds make up the only mixed assets category that's defined in SEC regulation: the SEC requires that a fund "which purports to be a 'balanced' fund should maintain at least 25%

of the value of its assets in fixed income senior securities" (that is, bonds and preferred stocks). They often have close to 40% in bonds and close to 60% in stocks.

Flexible portfolio funds, including asset allocation funds, differ from balanced funds in that their investment policies may give their managers more flexibility. Some are even permitted to concentrate 100% of their portfolios in one asset class, if they believe that would be appropriate.

Global flexible portfolio funds are very much like flexible portfolio funds except for one important difference: they are partially invested in foreign stocks, bonds, and money market instruments. To be so classified by Lipper, they must be at least 25% invested in securities traded outside the U.S.; some own a lot more.

Managers of income funds choose from among the three asset classes on the basis of the interest and dividend income they can be expected to produce. Inasmuch as the yields on the highest quality (triple-A) bonds have exceeded the yields on common stocks, as reflected by the S&P 500 Index, since 1958, you would expect that funds having income as their principal investment objective would tend to be primarily invested in bonds. The percentages of bonds owned by income funds vary a lot, though, as do the types of bonds they own. Their common stocks usually would have above-average yields; some might have below-average yields but have prospects for increased dividends.

Lipper has a separate category for a small number of income funds that are at least 85% invested in convertible and nonconvertible debt issues and preferred stocks, which it— ironically—calls flexible income funds. Because by definition such funds cannot invest more than 15% in common stocks, they would involve less stock market risk than income funds which may devote higher percentages of assets to stocks.

Why Invest in a Mixed Assets Fund

Think through why you would want to invest in a fund whose investment policy calls for it to own a mix of stocks, bonds, and money market instruments.

Is it for income? For total return? For preservation of principal? It wouldn't be primarily for capital appreciation; you would look to an equity fund for that. Also, would a mixed assets fund be your only fund?

> *tip* **Your Only Fund?** Because a mixed assets fund exposes you to both stock and bond market risk, be sure that you can live with the level of both types of risk that its investment policy would involve.

Your choice of a category, as well as of a fund within a category, should depend on how you answer these questions. If it's to be your only fund, make sure that it doesn't expose you to more market risk—whether stock market or bond market—than you are willing and able to accept.

When Income Is Your Principal Objective

If your principal investment objective is to receive current income, your choice of a mixed assets fund category would have to be between income and flexible income funds, the two that have distribution of income as their principal objective.

Their average yields run higher than those of the other mixed assets funds. As you may expect, their total returns, on the average, lag those of balanced and flexible portfolio funds.

Between income and flexible income funds, you may get more income from a leading flexible income fund for at least two reasons:

- It's probably more significantly invested in bonds.
- The bonds that it's invested in are more likely to be high-yield bonds.

To the extent that income funds are likely to own more common stocks that pay good dividends, they should have better prospects for appreciation.

Given the similar characteristics of the two categories, you might want to study leading funds in both and weigh how their investment policies square with your objectives and risk tolerance.

When Your Principal Objective Is Total Return

Balanced and flexible portfolio funds, including asset allocation funds, are more appropriate when your principal investment objective is total return.

Balanced funds also are likely to have the additional investment objectives of principal preservation and current income.

If the fund is to be your only mutual fund, a well-managed, balanced fund probably would be your best bet. You know it would have a minimum of 25% in fixed income securities to hold down the portfolio's volatility, and its asset allocation is likely to be relatively stable.

An asset allocation fund's investment policy may permit it to change allocations more radically, giving greater weight to the asset class that's expected to have a higher long-run return. If its securities selection doesn't involve excessive risks, it also might meet your requirements.

When you have picked out funds that have been above-average performers, for your analysis, here are some things to look for in each:

- Are its stated investment objectives compatible with yours?

- Are the asset allocations likely to be relatively stable, enabling you to expect relatively predictable returns over time, or are they likely to change a lot?

- Is the normal percentage of common stocks likely to be too low or too high for someone in your circumstances?

- If the fund has high current income as one of its stated objectives, is the statement matched by its dividend record?

- Does the fund usually invest in high- or low-quality bonds?

- If the stock portion is actively managed—that is, not linked to the S&P 500—what sorts of stocks does the fund usually own? Large-cap? Mid- and small-cap? Growth? Value? High- or low-dividend payers?

- Does the fund buy foreign bonds or stocks and, if so, do they constitute a significant share of the portfolio?

- Does the fund usually have more in cash equivalents than the minimum percentage of assets provided to meet possible redemption requests?

As you find the answers to these questions, it should become apparent which fund would be more appropriate for you.

In this lesson, you learned how to select a suitable mixed assets fund. In the next lesson, you learn how to read the prospectuses and shareholder reports that you get from fund companies.

16

Getting and Studying Information from Fund Companies

In this lesson, you learn what information to look for in the literature that you get from fund companies.

What a Fund Must Tell You

Of all the information about mutual funds that you may get from a variety of sources, nothing is as important—and as authoritative—as what you find in the prospectuses and shareholder reports that the companies themselves provide.

Federal laws and regulations require:

- That you be provided a current prospectus before you invest a cent in any money market, bond, or equity mutual fund, whether you deal directly with the fund company or indirectly through a broker or other salesperson.

- That you get its reports to shareholders at least semi-annually after you invest.

You should read at least certain portions of both when you get them and keep them for future reference.

Directors (or trustees) of a mutual fund are legally liable for the contents of its prospectus. This should assure you of the document's comprehensiveness and accuracy. It also assures you, unfortunately, of some tedious prose and ambiguities, which result from fund lawyers' determination to write the text in a way that complies with all the many applicable SEC rules while minimizing the risk of lawsuits—even if it may not comply with the SEC requirement that the information be "clear, concise and understandable."

A periodic shareholder report, too, must meet certain disclosure requirements. The financial statements in an annual report must be accompanied by a certificate of independent public accountants based on an audit.

Prospectus A pamphlet, which a mutual fund is legally required to make available to prospective investors, in which you can learn many things about the fund, including its investment objective and policies, the risks it incurs, the costs (if any) of buying or selling its shares, its annual operating expenses, its historic performance, and its manager.

Annual Report The report that a mutual fund must send its shareholders following the end of its fiscal year. It reviews the fund's performance during the year and provides audited financial statements as well as lists of the securities held by the fund at the year's end.

WHAT YOU SHOULD FOCUS ON IN A PROSPECTUS

The formats, contents, and readability of mutual fund prospectuses vary from company to company, but all are required by law or regulation to contain certain elements. They must be updated annually.

Of the elements common to prospectuses, the following are the most important ones for you to focus on.

INVESTMENT OBJECTIVE

In a brief paragraph on the cover and in more detail on ensuing pages, a prospectus must state its investment objective(s): whether the fund is primarily managed to achieve long-term capital appreciation, income (taxable or tax-exempt), total return, capital preservation, or a stable NAV (in the case of a money market fund). If income is a secondary objective, it will say so. If no consideration is given to income—that is, if the fund is invested in common stocks that pay low or no dividends—it should say that.

Be sure the stated investment objective is consistent with yours. Otherwise, the fund is unlikely to be suitable for you.

INVESTMENT POLICIES AND RISKS

This statement describes the policies that the fund follows to achieve its investment objective and notes the risks associated with them.

This section is must reading. It describes the securities in which the fund may be principally invested, any special investment techniques it employs, the industry or industries in which it is concentrated (if any), its use of securities denominated in foreign currencies, and the types of derivatives it employs.

If a fund's name implies that it will invest primarily in a particular type of security (other than money market instruments or tax-exempt bonds) or in a certain industry or industries, the SEC requires that its investment policy calls for its being invested at least 65% in the indicated types of securities or industries.

Unless the statement says so, you can't be sure, however, how the remaining 35% is likely to be invested during the years you own the fund.

If the statement in a bond, equity, or mixed assets fund prospectus indicates that its investment adviser has total discretion as to how much or how little he or she may invest in any securities or sectors, you can't be sure how 100% of the fund's assets will be invested.

As long as you can't be sure of how a fund will be invested—whether high- or low-risk stocks or bonds—you can't have a sense of its prospects for performance and its expected types and degrees of risk.

Shareholder Transaction Expenses

Right up front, you'll find a table, using the format of Table 16.1 as required by the SEC, which states what, if any, charges may be imposed when you buy or redeem a fund's shares.

Three patterns are the most common:

- *No-loads.* If you're considering a no-load fund whose shares you can buy or sell without a sales charge, the table will say "None" on every line—whether you're dealing directly with the fund sponsor or with a discount brokerage firm that has arranged with the

fund company to receive a share of the fees that it
receives annually from the fund.

TABLE 16.1   SHAREHOLDER TRANSACTION EXPENSES TABLE

Maximum sales load imposed on purchases (as a percentage of offering price)	_____%
Maximum sales load imposed on reinvested dividends (as a percentage of offering price)	_____%
Deferred sales load (as a percentage of original purchase price or redemption proceeds)	_____%
Redemption fees (as a percentage of amount redeemed, if applicable)	_____%
Exchange fee	_____%

Source: Form N-1A, U.S. Securities and Exchange Commission.

- *Front-end loads.* If a sales charge is imposed at the
  time of purchase, the table will quote the maximum
  rate, expressed as a percent of a fund's offering price,
  on the first line. A footnote or subsequent table may
  cite the lower rates charged for large investments. If a
  fund has more than one class of shares, the table
  would have a column of charges for each class; front-
  end loads would typically apply to its Class A shares.

Offering Price   The price at which shares of a
fund can be bought. For a fund with a front-end
load, it's defined as the net asset value (NAV) plus
the sales charge. For other funds, it's the same as
the NAV.

- *Back-end loads.* If a fund charges a load at the time of redemption—called a *deferred sales charge*—the table will state on the third line the rate imposed on redemptions within the first year. If it doesn't also do so, another part of the prospectus will give the schedule of declining rates for redemptions in following years, usually going out to the fifth or later year, when the charge is eliminated.

tip **No-Load or Not No-Load**   If anyone tries to persuade you that a fund with a deferred sales charge is a no-load fund because it imposes no front-end load, don't pay attention. It is a variety of load funds and cannot properly be regarded as no-load.

ANNUAL FUND OPERATING EXPENSES

The annual fund operating expenses table states the total operating expenses of a fund, expressed as a percent of its average net assets.

The SEC requires that operating expenses be broken into at least three broad categories:

- *Management fee.* This is the fee charged by the investment adviser for managing the fund's securities portfolio.

- *12b-1 fees.* These are charges imposed by many—but not all—funds in accordance with the SEC's Rule 12b-1 and with plans, approved by directors and shareholders, whereby fund assets may be tapped to compensate brokers and/or to finance other distribution costs.

The prospectus of a fund levying a 12b-1 fee must include a statement to the effect that long-term holders of its shares may pay more in 12b-1 fees than they would have paid if they had invested in shares with a front-end sales load.

> **-tip-** **12b-1 and No-Loads** If a fund imposes no front- or back-end sales load but does charge 12b-1 fees, it may be called a no-load fund only if those fees don't exceed 0.25%. No-load funds that don't impose 12b-1 fees are commonly called *pure no-load funds.*

- *Other expenses.* This item, which may be divided into three subcategories, includes all other costs that may be deducted from fund assets, such as payments to transfer agents, custodians, and other companies that provide services to the fund.

If a fund's expenses are temporarily reduced because fees are partially or even totally waived or reimbursed by its investment adviser, the prospectus must say so—and also tell you what the expenses would have been without the waiver or reimbursement.

MANAGEMENT

You'll want to know who the investment adviser is, how long the firm has acted in this capacity with the fund, who the portfolio manager is, and how long he or she has run the fund.

The SEC requires a statement citing the business experience during the past five years for every person "primarily responsible for the day-to-day management of the fund's portfolio" except for money market funds, index-matching funds, and funds managed by committees in cases where "no persons(s) is primarily responsible for making recommendations."

By determining how long an adviser and its portfolio manager(s) have run a fund, you'll learn whether this coincides with the period for which you've seen performance data that impressed you.

FINANCIAL HIGHLIGHTS

A table at the front of the prospectus provides certain financial data for the fund for the latest ten years—or for fewer years, if the fund hasn't been around that long.

The table shows you, among other things:

- How much the fund's NAV and annual total returns (not adjusted for a sales charge) have fluctuated over the period

- How much the fund has distributed in taxable or tax-exempt income and in capital gains (taxable each year, if you would have been invested in a taxable account)

- How much the ratios of the fund's operating expenses and net income to average net assets have gone up or down

- How high or low the fund's portfolio turnover rate has been (a possible—but not always reliable— indicator of the level of taxable capital gains)

If the investment adviser has changed during the period covered by the table, the SEC requires that a footnote must give the date of the change. There is no similar requirement for changes in portfolio managers.

OTHER INFORMATION

The prospectus also provides additional information that you
will need to know about a fund:

- *Minimum initial investment.* If a fund's minimum requirement exceeds the amount you have to invest,
  you may need to wait until you have more money or
  turn to another fund. Lower minimums may be
  available for IRAs and certain other accounts.

- *How to buy or sell shares.* In addition to information
  regarding the opening of an account with the fund
  company, securities dealers, or other firms, you'll
  find instructions on a variety of topics, including the
  uses of overnight express service, bank wire, check-
  writing, and automatic investment and withdrawal.

- *Distributions.* You'll learn when distributions of income and capital gains, if any, are scheduled.

WHAT YOU SHOULD FOCUS ON IN A REPORT TO SHAREHOLDERS

A periodic report to shareholders tells you how well or poorly
the fund performed during the most recent six or twelve
months, as well as what it was invested in as of the end of the
period.

MANAGEMENT DISCUSSION OF PERFORMANCE

Nothing is of more interest to you than the page or two of
discussion by the portfolio manager about the factors that
significantly affected the fund's performance, including conditions in the markets in which the fund was invested and the
strategies that he or she pursued.

Whatever merit other comments on the economy or other topics may have, they aren't as important to you as the forthright, comprehensive analysis of the fund's performance—especially following a period when securities prices dropped.

LINE GRAPH

Be sure to glance at a line graph (which also may appear in the prospectus) in which the fund's performance over the latest ten years is compared with that of an appropriate broad-based securities market index, picked by the fund company in compliance with an SEC requirement.

It will quickly tell you how you would have fared by being invested in the fund, inasmuch as the data have to reflect any sales charges that would have been imposed, and how well the manager picked securities out of the stock or bond universes in which the fund was and remains invested.

PERFORMANCE TABLE

Along with the line graph, you should find a table providing the fund's average annual returns for the latest one, five, and ten years, also calculated to reflect any sales charges, as well as the average returns for the same index chosen for the chart.

FINANCIAL HIGHLIGHTS

A financial highlights table, similar to that of the prospectus, will bring you up-to-date on data such as distributions, operating expenses, and portfolio turnover.

Portfolio Characteristics

You have no real need to study the list of securities in the
fund's portfolio at the end of the reporting period, partly
because you may not have the time to analyze their appropri-
ateness and to second-guess the manager and partly because
some of the securities may already have been sold and re-
placed.

What you do want to see, however, are some of the data that
reveal the portfolio's characteristics so that you can reassure
yourself of the fund's suitability for you:

- How the assets were allocated among stocks, bonds,
  and money market instruments

- How much the fund was concentrated in its top ten
  stock or bond holdings

- How the portfolio was concentrated in industries or
  other sectors of the stock or bond markets and, in
  the case of foreign securities, among foreign markets

- For bond funds, the distribution of the portfolio's
  bonds by credit quality ratings, its weighted average
  maturity, and, perhaps, duration

In this lesson, you learned what information to look for in the
literature that you get from fund companies. In the next lesson, you learn about the costs of buying and owning mutual
funds—and how to keep them down.

THE COSTS OF BUYING AND OWNING MUTUAL FUNDS

In this lesson, you learn about the costs of buying and owning mutual funds—and how to keep them down.

TYPES OF COSTS

When you invest in mutual funds, you incur one or two types of costs. One, a sales charge, or "load," may be taken out of your investment when you buy shares in an equity, bond, or mixed assets fund, or it may be taken out of your proceeds when you sell.

The other is your share of the costs of operating a fund, which you absorb year after year as long as you are invested in it.

You can avoid the one-time sales charge, if you choose to buy a no-load fund directly from a fund company. You can't avoid annual operating expenses—except for a few funds whose investment advisers are temporarily waiving or reimbursing them—but you can look for funds whose managements try to keep them down.

WHY YOU WOULD BUY NO-LOAD FUNDS FROM FUND COMPANIES

You would buy directly marketed no-load funds from the fund companies that sponsor them because it should be more profitable for you to do so.

If two funds—a load fund and a no-load fund—have identical portfolios and annual operating expense ratios and are managed the same way, the no-load fund has to provide you with a higher return on your investment. When you invest in the no-load fund, all your money is working for you.

 Another No-Load Advantage A no-load fund would have an even greater advantage over a load fund than indicated by the sales charge, if the load fund has higher annual operating expenses.

WHY YOU MIGHT USE A DISCOUNT BROKER FOR NO-LOADS

You might wish to consider buying no-load funds through a discount broker, provided that (1) you could do so without paying a sales commission or transaction fee and (2) you would absorb no higher annual expenses than if you dealt directly with the fund sponsors.

Why would you do so? If you want to invest in two or more funds offered by two or more companies and you would like the advantages of dealing with only one organization: less paperwork and easier switches between different companies' funds, for example.

A disadvantage would be that you would not have direct communication with the sponsors of the directly marketed funds that you invest in.

LOADS, NO-LOADS, AND PERFORMANCE

Regardless of what a salesperson may tell you, there is no reason to believe that a load fund managed to achieve your investment objective would outperform a no-load fund managed equally well to achieve a similar objective and incurring the same level of risk. Or vice versa.

There are superior—and inferior—funds in both categories.

Sales loads have nothing to do with how well a portfolio manager performs. They do not provide him or her an incentive to perform better. Receipts from loads go to the fund distributor, securities dealer, broker, and others involved in the marketing of fund shares. On the other hand, loads do have an impact on what you earn on your investment: they reduce it.

WHY YOU WOULD BUY FROM A BROKER OR OTHER SALESPERSON

You would buy shares of a load fund from a broker, financial planner, or other salesperson because you don't have the time or interest in acquiring the knowledge necessary to perform your own research and make your own fund selections. You may lack self-confidence when it comes to handling large sums of money and may find it overwhelming to deal with the challenge of investing in a way that assures you not only of avoiding a serious loss but also of maintaining your standard of living when you retire. These are, of course, understandable considerations.

Under the circumstances, you would have to be willing to pay the costs associated with load funds—even if they eat into your returns—so that you can benefit from the advice of competent professionals to which a sales charge should entitle you.

WHAT YOU NEED TO DO WHEN BUYING LOAD FUNDS

Even though you are willing to pay sales charges for professional advice when buying load funds, you should still not be a passive investor and simply agree to anything and everything a salesperson recommends. You should understand enough about the likely long-run returns and risks associated with financial asset classes so that you can affirm for yourself the asset allocation that's recommended to you. You should also understand enough about the likely long-run performance and risks of mutual funds so that you can affirm the suitability of the funds recommended for your investment.

ALL ABOUT OPERATING EXPENSES

The SEC requires every mutual fund's prospectus to disclose its expenses, as percentages of average net assets over the most recent 12-month period, in three broad categories and in total, in the format that you see in Table 17.1.

TABLE 17.1 ANNUAL FUND OPERATING EXPENSES (AS A PERCENTAGE OF AVERAGE NET ASSETS)

OPERATING EXPENSES	PERCENTAGE OF AVERAGE NET ASSETS
Management fees	_____%
12b-1 fees	_____%

OPERATING EXPENSES	PERCENTAGE OF AVERAGE NET ASSETS
Other expenses	_____%
Total fund operating expenses	_____%

Source: Form N-1A, U.S. Securities and Exchange Commission.

The percentage that total operating expenses represent of a fund's average net assets is commonly referred to as the *expense ratio.*

 Expense Ratio   The ratio of a fund's annual operating expenses to its average net assets over the period. It usually shouldn't exceed 1%. Low-cost, truly investor-friendly funds may have ratios of 0.5% or even less.

MANAGEMENT FEES

These consist primarily of the investment advisory fee paid to the fund's investment adviser to manage the portfolio and may also take in any other management or administrative fees.

Investment advisory contracts between the fund and its adviser may stipulate that the fee be based on a flat percentage of a fund's average net assets, regardless of its size, or on a schedule of rates that decline as a fund's assets grow.

In a minority of cases, the basic fee is supplemented by a performance adjustment—an additional sum for performance above a relevant securities price index, or a reduction for performance below that standard. The Standard & Poor's 500 Index is commonly used for equity funds.

Lipper calculated the median management fee for general equity funds at about 0.7%. World equity funds, whose management usually necessitates higher outlays for securities research and other activities abroad, cost slightly more to run. Mixed assets, sector, bond, and money market funds cost less.

12B-1 FEES

The most controversial annual expenses that mutual fund managements impose on their shareholders are 12b-1 fees.

Named for a rule that the SEC adopted in 1980, 12b-1 fees may be charged by funds whose directors and shareholders have approved plans permitting fund assets to be tapped for money to finance distribution costs to attract additional investors. Outlays could include the costs of advertising, payments to brokers or dealers, and prospectuses for other than current shareholders.

The theory is that current shareholders should be willing to pay to attract additional investors in the hope that, as a fund grows and its fixed costs are spread across a larger asset base, per-share costs should be reduced for everybody's benefit. This has not been convincingly proven.

Load funds tend to use 12b-1 fees to a large extent to compensate brokers and other salespeople, giving them an incentive not merely to sell their shares and to hold customers' hands, so to speak, during the years they own them but especially to sell shares with back-end loads.

Because back-end-load shares can be bought at their NAVs, they are more easily sold. But, because they are bought without the one-time front-end loads out of which brokers are ordinarily paid, they also tend to have higher 12b-1 fees than front-end-load funds—and, thus, higher annual income for those who sell them.

The pervasiveness of 12b-1 fees is striking. Around 60% of funds or share classes in every broad fund category had adopted 12b-1 plans when Lipper checked in early 1996—even nearly 60% of retail money market funds, whose shareholders presumably require less hand holding than those of aggressive growth funds.

Of course, the median fees are striking, too, ranging from 0.20% for money market funds to 0.75% for considerably riskier sector funds.

OTHER EXPENSES

The remaining categories of expenses tend to involve less money and less controversy. They include fees for custodians, who hold fund assets; transfer agents, who maintain shareholders' records; independent public accountants, who conduct the necessary audits; lawyers, who deal with regulation, litigation, and legislation; independent directors; and the costs of printing, postage, and a variety of other items.

TOTAL OPERATING EXPENSES

When you add up all the expenses, they amount to a considerable amount of money: a median of about 1.3% for general equity funds, more for sector and world equity funds, nearly 1% for domestic bond funds. Moreover, Lipper has observed that total operating expenses have been rising as percentages of net assets, even as total assets have experienced a noteworthy increase.

In this lesson, you learned about the costs of buying and owning mutual funds—and how to keep them down. In the next lesson, you learn some investment techniques and strategies.

18

SOME
INVESTMENT
STRATEGIES AND
TECHNIQUES

In this lesson, you learn some investment strategies and techniques.

LUMP-SUM INVESTING VERSUS DOLLAR-COST AVERAGING

Having selected the equity, bond, and/or money market funds that you want to invest in—based on your own research or on the recommendation of a broker or advisor—you may want to think about the ways in which you put your money to work. Perhaps the first decision you'll face is whether to invest a lump sum of money all at once in an equity or bond fund or to invest fixed amounts at regular intervals, a practice known as *dollar-cost averaging*.

Dollar-cost averaging is a useful, disciplined form of investing in a mutual fund. It takes at least some of the emotion and guesswork out of investing by obliging you to invest regularly, regardless of whether the markets are placid or turbulent and regardless of how you might feel about either situation.

When securities prices are down, you pick up more shares with the same amount of money. When they're up, you naturally pick up fewer shares. If, for example, you have $200 taken out monthly, and a fund's NAV is $20, you get 10 shares. If the NAV goes, say, to $21, you will get 9.524 shares. On the other hand, if it should slip to $19, you'd get 10.526.

> *tip* **Automatic Investment** If you want to invest a sum regularly in a mutual fund outside a company plan, you may be able to authorize the fund company to withdraw a set amount regularly from your bank account. Some companies permit you to invest as little as $50 or $100.

By practicing dollar-cost averaging for a number of years, you may be able to have a lower average cost than if you invest a lump sum, and ultimately have a larger capital gain—maybe. It depends, of course, on what securities do during the period that you're invested, the sizes and timing of the distributions that you invest, and whether securities prices have been rising or falling when you want to sell.

Handling a Lump Sum from Your Employer

The largest sum of money that you will ever get your hands on may be the sum distributed to you out of your employer's retirement or savings plan when you retire, early or at the "normal" age of 65, or when you leave your employer voluntarily or involuntarily for other reasons.

Because whether you have a comfortable retirement may depend on what you do with the money, you will want to handle it very carefully. That means that you will want to be mindful of both income tax and investment considerations.

Depending on what income tax regulations stipulate at the time, on whether you plan to go to work for another employer, and on what that employer's plan permits, you may determine that it would be most advantageous to roll over the sum from your plan tax-free into one or more IRAs. If you do, and the income tax regulations remain unchanged, you will be able to do so, provided that you meet two conditions:

- You move the money within 60 days of receiving the distribution.

- You don't actually lay your hands on the money but have your plan's trustee move the money to an IRA's trustee. Otherwise, you would be subject to a withholding tax of 20%.

Being prudent and concerned about investment risk, you would not want to commit all the money into one equity or bond fund at one time. Yet, the 60-day rule necessitates your moving quickly, and your plan trustee's policy probably provides for issuing only one check, instead of a number of checks that could accommodate your desire for diversification.

What do you do?

1. Choose at least one mutual fund family in whose equity and/or bond fund(s) you want to invest.

2. Obtain a prospectus at least for that group's money market fund, as well as the forms necessary to enable you to open a rollover IRA account in that fund.

3. Authorize your plan trustee to move all your distribution into the money market fund.

After your money is safely out of your plan administrator's hands and the IRS's clutches, you can deliberately implement your investment strategy at your own speed, investing your distribution—in lumps or installments—in as many or as few funds as you want.

Using the proper forms, you can easily ask the trustee of your initial IRA to transfer whatever you want to the trustees for the other groups' equity and/or bond fund(s) that you have designated for your long-term investment.

> **-tip-** **Comply with the 60-Day Rule**   Don't take lightly the IRS's ability to withhold 20% of the distribution from your qualified retirement plan, if you don't move it directly to an IRA within the permitted 60 days. Make sure that the money reaches its destination on time.

Allocating Among Taxable, Tax-Exempt, and Tax-Deferred Accounts

If you're like many other people, regardless of age or financial circumstances, you are likely, or expect, to have money invested in mutual fund accounts with three different types of taxability status: fully taxable, tax-exempt, and tax-deferred.

Against this background, try to allocate your assets and deploy your money within asset classes so that you give maximum consideration to potential taxes.

Money Market Funds

Unless you're investing in a tax-deferred account, keep in mind your federal income tax bracket and determine whether a tax-exempt money market fund would provide you more income than you would have left after federal and state taxes on a taxable money market fund. If a taxable fund is only invested in money market instruments issued by the Treasury, its income distributions may be exempt from your state income tax. For a tax-deferred account, you would only want a taxable money market fund.

BOND FUNDS

With your federal tax bracket in mind, follow the same guidelines as in the preceding paragraph with respect to choosing between taxable and tax-exempt funds that are likely to have similar—and appropriate—levels of interest rate and credit risk.

If a tax-deferred account is available to you, you may want to use it for investment in a higher-yielding fund, such as a junk bond fund or a long-term investment grade bond fund.

EQUITY FUNDS

The same rationale applies to decisions regarding equity funds. To the extent possible, use your tax-deferred account(s) for equity funds that are likely to pay higher dividends and capital gains distributions and less likely to be volatile and result in capital losses.

If you can accept the risks associated with them—in the hope of earning higher returns—you may want to use taxable accounts for relatively volatile equity funds that pay low or no dividends and may have low or infrequent capital gains distributions. Investing in such funds may raise the possibility that you could suffer some capital losses if you should have or want to sell, but you could reduce their impact by using them to offset some of your other income on your tax return.

MAXIMIZING RETURNS BY MINIMIZING TAXES

When you're investing in equity funds in taxable accounts, you want to maximize your returns by minimizing taxes on income and capital gains distributions.

To minimize taxes on income, you have to select funds that tend to pay low or no taxable dividends. This does involve certain risk, however, because such funds sometimes may be more volatile than dividend-paying funds and, therefore, could expose you to the possibility of having to sell at a loss.

Minimizing taxes on capital gains distributions is more of a challenge, because you can't always tell ahead of time when a fund is likely to declare such distributions and how large they are likely to be.

You may get clues from two lines in the financial highlights table in a fund's prospectus or report to shareholders:

- The capital gains that the fund distributed in the past give you an idea of its tendency to declare them and of their size in relation to its NAV at the time.

- The fund's portfolio turnover rate may indicate the frequency with which the portfolio manager trades securities.

But, naturally, you have to remember that these are historic data. You have no guarantee that past patterns will continue. A portfolio manager may decide to recast his or her portfolio, replacing so many securities that capital gains may be generated at an above-average rate for the fund.

In this lesson, you learned about some investment strategies and techniques. In the next lesson, you learn how to monitor your funds' performance.

MONITORING YOUR FUNDS' PERFORMANCE

In this lesson, you learn how to monitor the performance of your equity or bond funds to watch for slippage.

CHECKING FUND PERFORMANCE

Whether you invested in funds on your own or through a broker, you should monitor them periodically to see whether they are performing as well as or worse than you expected.

Even if you have paid a sales charge and are absorbing annual 12b-1 fees to compensate a broker so that he or she will keep you informed, you may have to check on how your funds are doing so that you can be sure that your portfolio is on track.

HOW OFTEN TO CHECK ON YOUR FUNDS

If you are well invested, thanks to your own research or to good advice, you don't have to rush for your newspaper's fund price tables every morning to see how your funds did the previous day.

If you are a long-term investor, day-to-day changes should be of little or no interest to you, unless they are unusually large and are the consequence of a major development, such as a change in the Federal Reserve's monetary policy. Even then, you may not have to take any action.

When you own a mutual fund, you are paying a professional manager to manage a portfolio of securities for you. Let him or her worry about the daily activity of the stock or bond market and whether certain securities should be bought or sold.

If you have the time over the weekend, you may want to look at your newspaper's weekend fund tables or at *Barron's* to see how your funds performed during the week, especially if there was a significant change of, say, 2% or more in the stock or bond market.

If you don't have the time or the interest to check funds weekly and if prices in the securities markets are fluctuating more or less within a narrow range, it would be a good idea to check on your funds every three months. Unless you own a fund that voluntarily publishes a quarterly report to shareholders, you will probably find the special quarterly sections published by *Barron's* or *The Wall Street Journal* useful.

At the very least, check on your funds every six months, when you receive the mandated semiannual or annual reports to shareholders from the funds.

What to Look For

Let's assume that you're looking at a quarterly review of your funds' performance. You should look at:

- Your funds' absolute performance
- Your funds' relative performance

ABSOLUTE PERFORMANCE

You want to know the total returns that each of your funds achieved in the latest three-month period, as well as in the latest 12-month and other periods, so that you can get a sense of whether each one is maintaining the rate of performance that you expect of it over the long term.

By doing a little sharp-pencil work, you can figure out the combined performance of all your funds so that you will know whether your total portfolio is maintaining the pace that you're depending on to meet your investment goal.

RELATIVE PERFORMANCE

Important as total return data for individual funds may be in indicating funds' absolute performance, they are not enough. Total return data do not tell you whether your funds performed as well as you had reason to expect, which you can ascertain by comparing your funds' data with the performance of securities price indexes reflecting the market sectors in which they are invested and the performance of competing funds with similar investment objectives.

If a fund went up, you'll want to get a sense of whether it rose as much as it might have. You want to benefit as much as possible from the lift that an up phase in the markets can provide.

If a fund went down, as can happen to the best of them, you'll want to get a sense of whether it went down more than it should have, considering how you expected the fund to be invested and how it actually was invested (that is, its asset allocation and its manager's selection of higher-risk and lower-risk stocks or bonds).

The most important bases for determining relative performance are the total returns for the stock and bond indexes that fund managements have designated as appropriate benchmarks for their funds, in accordance with SEC requirements. You'll find them identified in the funds' prospectuses and/or shareholder reports.

If a fund publishes a quarterly report to shareholders, you'll find a comparison of its performance for the latest quarter, year, and, perhaps, other periods with that of its benchmark index. If a fund does not publish a quarterly, you'll need to refer to *The Wall Street Journal*, *Barron's*, *Morningstar Mutual Funds*, or other publications.

tip **Note the Company a Fund Keeps**   When you compare a fund's performance with that of its peer group, be sure to compare it with the same peer group consistently. Lipper, Morningstar, and others classify funds differently. It can be confusing to go back and forth among peer groups.

You should compare the funds' quarterly performance with peer funds in its investment objective categories, such as those calculated by Lipper. You can find such comparisons in quarterly fund reports or in newspapers or business magazines.

CDA/Wiesenberger's *Mutual Funds Report*, *Morningstar Mutual Funds*, and *The Value Line Mutual Fund Survey* also publish performance data for investment objective categories, but they classify funds differently so you may be a bit confused if you are accustomed to Lipper's classification system.

ANALYZING AND ACTING ON THE DATA

What do you do with the data?

When comparing your funds' total returns with those of their benchmark indexes and peer group averages, see whether the funds have been consistently beating both—whether rising more or falling less—including the most recent period.

If all your funds have done so, you can stop your analysis, congratulate yourself, and relax—until next time.

If a fund has begun to lag both its benchmark and its group average, study its shareholder report for an explanation. If management's discussion of its performance is plausible and you have reason to expect improvement, you'll probably want to be patient and not do anything. If, however, the fund has been lagging both for several quarters—say, four or more—you will want to find out why this has been going on. Read the fund's report to shareholders and, if it is not informative, call the fund (or ask the broker or other salesperson who recommended it to you).

You can, of course, read *Morningstar's* or *Value Line's* analysis of the fund's performance, but you should be able to get a forthright explanation from the fund. Its management owes it to you and your fellow shareholders.

If the explanation doesn't satisfy you and you don't expect the performance to improve, consider switching out of the fund into one in the same category with a better record and better prospects—provided that a leading fund in the group would still be appropriate for you.

If management's explanation is not forthcoming or not forthright, you won't want to take much time to decide to switch.

If a fund has been beating its peer group but lagging its benchmark index by more than its expense ratio—because indexes are unmanaged, they involve no management fees—you may have reason to expect better performance of the fund.

> *tip* **A Meaningful Standard**   The securities price index that a fund's management designates as an appropriate benchmark for comparing its performance is a meaningful standard. The management fee that you pay should reward you with superior performance. Otherwise, you might as well invest in a fund that's managed to match the index.

The category may be comprised of funds with lackluster performance records, whereas the index provides a more meaningful standard. See whether management adequately explains why it lags the index which, after all, it had designated as an appropriate benchmark.

When you are invested in a fund that has allocated assets to all three major classes—stocks, bonds, and cash—you can easily compare its performance to others in the same category, but you can't use a single index for a meaningful comparison of its performance. If you're lucky, the fund's shareholder report may have created a hypothetical index that's weighted among asset classes in the same way as the portfolio. Otherwise, if you have a knack for numbers, you could create your own.

YOUR SUPPLEMENTARY READING

If you have the time and the interest, you can keep up with your funds by reading what you can find in newspapers, magazines, and newsletters in addition to the material that you get from the funds and that you see in *Morningstar* or *Value Line*.

Be alert for news of changes in portfolio managers, which you should read about in prospectuses and shareholder reports and which you may read about in periodicals.

Also, look for news of changes in a fund's investment objective and/or investment policy, which you may read about in a shareholder report or letter from the fund or in a fund proxy statement, if the subject is one on which you and other shareholders are asked to vote.

If you're confused by literature from a fund, or if you have a question about something you read elsewhere, don't hesitate to call the fund company to get the information. You should expect to get an adequate response.

In this lesson, you learned how to monitor the performance of your funds periodically to watch for slippage. In the next lesson, you learn about switching funds as you become older or as your circumstances change.

SWITCHING FUNDS BECAUSE OF YOUR AGE OR CHANGED CIRCUMSTANCES

In this lesson, you learn some things to consider when it becomes appropriate to switch funds as you get older or as your circumstances change.

REASONS TO SWITCH FUNDS OTHER THAN POOR PERFORMANCE

You learned about switching out of funds when they don't perform as well as you expected or as well as you require to meet your investment goals. However, funds don't have to perform poorly for you to switch out of them.

WHEN YOUR INVESTMENT HORIZON CHANGES AS YOU GET OLDER

If you had a long investment horizon when you first invested in funds, you probably (and correctly) assumed that you could accept a high level of risk. You knew that you could take turbulence in the stock and bond markets in stride because you could ride out the market ups and downs over time.

Probably, you elected to allocate the largest chunk of your financial assets to equity funds, a small percentage to bond funds, and almost nothing to a money market fund. You tended to invest the equity portion more in aggressive equity funds, such as capital appreciation (or aggressive growth) and growth, and the bond portion in long-term taxable or tax-exempt bond funds. You knew that these funds were likely to be fairly volatile, but you didn't mind because you expected above-average returns along with above-average risks.

However, as you get older, approaching retirement and certainly when you're entering retirement, it makes sense for you to gradually moderate the level of risk of your funds.

Adjusting Your Asset Allocation

The first step is to adjust your asset allocation by reducing the percentage of your portfolio that is invested in equity funds and increasing the percentage that is in bond funds as well, perhaps, as the percentage that is in a money market fund.

How should your assets be allocated when you're planning to retire in the next three or four years?

If, say, you're in your mid-50s and expect to retire at age 65, you might want to think about switching from 75% or more in equity funds toward 50% to 60% or so, allocating the remainder to bond funds. If you are within a few years of retirement, you might move to a more conservative allocation—perhaps 45% to 50% in equity funds.

Whatever you do, unless your situation is unusual, it probably would be imprudent to get out of equity and bond funds com-

20

pletely to switch all your money to a money market fund. You can't be sure that the money market fund will protect you adequately against inflation. Even when you're retired and aged, you'll probably want to have roughly 20% of your holdings in equity funds and much of the rest in bond funds.

Adjusting Your Fund Mix

After you've decided on your asset allocation for the next few years, you can consider how to adjust your fund mixes gradually within the asset classes.

If you are only invested in more volatile equity funds, it would be a good idea to begin to reduce your risk level by gradually moving to less volatile funds in the growth & income and equity income categories. You probably want to switch from below-average-yield to above-average-yield equity funds.

If your bond funds have only been the more volatile ones— long-term funds involving higher interest rate risk and/or high-yield funds involving higher credit risk—you might consider reducing the levels of the risks to which you are exposed by moving into intermediate- or short-term funds and/or higher-grade bond funds, respectively.

When Your Investment Horizon Contracts Because of Circumstances

You don't have to be nearing retirement to have a slowly shrinking investment horizon. You can be at the start or in the middle of a career, accumulating money to provide for your children's college education, to buy a first house or a vacation house, or to buy a business or farm, while saving for your far-off retirement at the same time.

Whatever your circumstances, the same principles apply as when you're older, even if you do have one major advantage: confidence that most of your income will continue to be derived from your work, and probably to rise with inflation, instead of from investments whose market values and income distributions can fluctuate.

As the time when you need the money for tuition or a major purchase gets closer, you do the same two things: adjust the asset allocation of the investment accounts dedicated to this purpose by reducing the equity and/or bond fund portions, as appropriate, while raising the money market fund portions and by moving gradually from higher-risk to lower-risk equity and/or bond funds.

Because you are likely to be in a medium- or high-income tax bracket if you're in mid-career, you will, of course, want to take into consideration the potential income tax consequences of any switches. If your investments have appreciated considerably since you bought them, you will want to weigh the possible tax on your capital gains against the possibility that the values of your investments (and, thus, your capital gains) could drop.

A low-yielding money market fund may seem unattractive after years in which you have earned higher returns in equity and bond funds, but it is safer and, therefore, better than the alternatives. You don't want to take a chance that you won't have the money when you want it, especially when your children are ready to go to college.

When Your Investment Horizon Becomes Uncertain

You face an especially difficult challenge if your investment horizon has become—or may become—uncertain because you have lost your job, you are concerned that you may lose it in the near future, or a family member has become seriously ill, requiring major medical expenses for an unpredictable period.

> **Don't Panic**   Whatever you do when you lose your job, don't panic and abandon your well-considered investments. Analyze your situation to determine the alternatives available to you; calmly think through a suitable strategy and then deliberately implement it. Acting in panic could cost you money unnecessarily just when you can least afford it.

What you don't want to do when your investment horizon becomes uncertain for these or other reasons is panic, sell everything—possibly having to pay income tax on capital gains just when you need cash—and move all your money into a money market fund.

You may eventually wind up doing that, but you should not do it without first taking stock of your investments and doing some deliberate planning.

As you analyze your situation, you may find it appropriate to take steps such as the following:

- Figure out how much cash you could easily withdraw from money market funds and other accounts without the possibility of incurring income taxes on capital gains or other costs.

- If you're in a tax-exempt money market fund and are likely to be in a lower income tax bracket because of your job loss, calculate whether your after-tax income from a taxable money market fund would be higher and, therefore, would make a non-taxable switch desirable.

- Estimate how long you and your family could live on your easily available cash reserves (plus any other income, such as unemployment compensation or severance pay).

- Add up your investments in taxable and/or tax-exempt accounts and get a rough idea of the taxable capital gains and capital losses that you would realize if you had to sell them.

- Depending on how much cash you can easily access without having to pay taxes and how much money you are likely to need to live on, determine how much of your other taxable and tax-exempt investments you may need to liquidate.

- Figure out how your combined financial assets—taxable, tax-exempt, and tax-deferred accounts—are allocated and decide how you think they ought to be allocated after effecting the liquidations of investments that could become necessary. In all likelihood, you will want to have a less risky allocation until you are more assured about your financial outlook.

- Rank the candidates for possible sales after giving proper consideration to the tax consequences, to your asset allocation, and to your need for adequate diversification. You may want first to sell positions in which you have capital losses that could be offset against other income (up to IRS's $3,000 annual limit) and then sell those in which you have unrealized taxable capital gains. Alternatively, you might consider matching sales of shares on which you have unrealized capital losses with those on which you have unrealized gains.

• If you have lost your job, or are about to, and expect to work again for somebody else, consider the feasibility and desirability of leaving your tax-deferred retirement account's balance with your old employer while conducting your job search. If it isn't feasible or desirable—and if you aren't going to need the money to live on—become prepared to roll over your balance tax-free into an IRA.

In this lesson, you learned the factors involved when you're considering switching funds as you get older or as your circumstances change.

Now that you've completed the book, you know whether investing in mutual funds would be right for you and, if so, which categories of funds would be most appropriate, how you go about selecting the most suitable funds within the categories, and how to monitor them to be sure they live up to your expectations.

In other words, you have the basic tools to be your own money manager—to plan a strategy consistent with your needs and tolerance of investment risk, to implement that strategy, and, if and when it becomes necessary, to change it.

You won't get rich overnight, but if you plan your strategy on the basis of realistic expectations and stick with it—turning a deaf ear to voices of both euphoria and despair—you have a good chance of realizing your investment goals.

May you do so in the best of health.